A PRISON DIARY

VOLUME TWO – WAYLAND: PURGATORY

'Archer paints a bleak but true picture of life in prison
. . . it is vivid and disturbing, and will reach a vastly wider
audience than any academic treatise or political pamphlet
on the subject' – Ann Widdecombe, *New Statesman*

'Pick this up and be amazed and absorbed by Archer's
best bit of writing by far . . . this is compelling stuff,
well worth reading – and deserving of some
serious attention' – *Manchester Evening News*

'A monument to the stiff upper lip' – *Observer*

During his incarceration Jeffrey Archer wrote three volumes of prison diaries:

Volume One – Belmarsh: Hell

Volume Two – Wayland: Purgatory

Volume Three – North Sea Camp: Heaven

Since being released, Jeffrey has written his first screenplay, *Mallory: Walking off the Map*, run the London Marathon (slowly) and begun work on a new novel.

By the same author

FF 8282

A PRISON DIARY

VOLUME TWO – WAYLAND: PURGATORY

PAN BOOKS

First published 2003 by Macmillan

This edition published 2004 by Pan Books
an imprint of Pan Macmillan Ltd
Pan Macmillan, 20 New Wharf Road, London N1 9RR
Basingstoke and Oxford
Associated companies throughout the world
www.panmacmillan.com

ISBN 0 330 41884 X

A CIP catalogue record for this book is available from
the British Library.

Typeset by SetSystems Ltd, Saffron Walden, Essex
Printed and bound in Great Britain by
Mackays of Chatham plc, Chatham, Kent

All Pan Macmillan titles are available from
www.panmacmillan.com
or from Bookpost by telephoning 01624 677237

THE THOUSANDTH MAN

One man in a thousand, Solomon says,
Will stick more close than a brother.
And it's worth while seeking him half your days
If you find him before the other.
Nine hundred and ninety-nine depend
On what the world sees in you,
But the Thousandth Man will stand your friend
With the whole round world agin you.

'Tis neither promise nor prayer nor show
Will settle the finding for 'ee
Nine hundred and ninety-nine of 'em go
By your looks, or your acts, or your glory.
But if he finds you and you find him,
The rest of the world don't matter;
For the Thousandth Man will sink or swim
With you in any water.

You can use his purse with no more talk
Than he uses yours for his spendings,
And laugh and meet in your daily walk
As though there had been no lendings.
Nine hundred and ninety-nine of 'em call
For silver and gold in their dealings;
But the Thousandth Man he's worth 'em all,
Because you can show him your feelings.

His wrong's your wrong, and his right's your right,
In season or out of season.
Stand up and back it in all men's sight –
With *that* for your only reason!
Nine hundred and ninety-nine can't bide
The shame or mocking or laughter,
But the Thousandth Man will stand by your side
To the gallows-foot – and after!

Rudyard Kipling (1865–1936)

To Mary

The thousandth woman

DAY 22   THURSDAY 9 AUGUST 2001

10.21 am

It is a glorious day: a day for watching cricket, for drinking Pimm's, for building sandcastles, for mowing the lawn. Not a day to be travelling in a sweatbox for 120 miles.

Having served twenty-one days and fourteen hours in Belmarsh, I am about to be transported to HMP Wayland, a Category C prison in Norfolk. A Group 4 van is my chauffeur-driven transport, with two cubicles for two prisoners.* I remain locked in for fifteen minutes awaiting the arrival of a second prisoner. I hear him talking, but can't see him. Is he also going to Wayland?

At last the great electric gates of Belmarsh slide open and we begin our journey east. My temporary moving residence is a compartment four feet by three with a plastic seat. I feel nauseous within ten minutes, and am covered in sweat within fifteen.

The journey to Wayland prison in Norfolk takes just over

---

* As I explained in *Volume One* of these diaries, there are four categories of prisoner: A, B, C, D. A-cat are violent and dangerous prisoners, with the possible resources (i.e. money) to escape; B-cat are violent and dangerous, but not always murderers: they might be in for GBH, ABH, manslaughter or rape, or have already served five years in an A-cat; in C-cats, the vast majority are repeat offenders or convicted of a serious, non-violent crime (i.e. drug-dealing); D-cats are usually for first offenders with no history of violence, who are likely to conform to the system, as they wish to return to society as quickly as possible.

three hours. As I peer through my tiny window I recognize the occasional familiar landmark on the Cambridge leg of the trip. Once the university city is behind us, I have to satisfy myself with a glimpse at signposts whenever we slow down at roundabouts to pinpoint where we are: Newmarket, Bury St Edmunds, Thetford. So for this particular period of my life that very special lady, Gillian Shephard, will be my Member of Parliament.

The roads become narrower and the trees taller the further east we travel. When we finally arrive at Wayland it couldn't be in starker contrast to the entrance of Belmarsh with its foreboding high walls and electric gates. And – most pleasing of all – not a member of the press in sight. We drive into the yard and come to a halt outside the reception area. I sense immediately a different atmosphere and a more casual approach by prison officers. But then their daily tariff is not gangland murderers, IRA terrorists, rapists and drug barons.

The first officer I meet as I walk into reception is Mr Knowles. Once he has completed the paperwork, he signs me over to a Mr Brown, as if I were a registered parcel. Once again, I am strip-searched before the officer empties my HMP Belmarsh plastic bag onto the counter and rummages through my possessions. He removes my dressing gown, the two large blue towels William had so thoughtfully supplied and a blue tracksuit. He informs me that they will be returned to me as soon as I am enhanced.*

'How long will that take?' I ask.

'Usually about three months,' he replies casually, as if it were

---

* Every prisoner begins life as standard and then, according to his behaviour, moves up or down. There are three levels of status: basic, standard and enhanced – and in some prisons, super-enhanced. Enhanced prisoners are afforded extra privileges. They are allowed to wear their own clothes, have longer periods out of their cell, have two extra visits per month and another £5 a week added to their weekly canteen account. So it's well worth becoming enhanced as quickly as possible.

a few grains of sand passing through an hourglass. I don't think I'll mention to Mr Brown that I'm hoping to be moved within a few days, once the police enquiry into Baroness Nicholson's complaint concerning the Simple Truth appeal has been seen for what it is.*

Mr Brown then places my beige slacks and blue shirt on one side, explaining that I won't get those back until I've been released or transferred. He replaces them with a striped blue prison shirt and a pair of jeans. After signing over my personal possessions, my photograph is taken, holding up a little blackboard with the chalk letters FF 8282 under my chin, just as you've seen in films.

I am escorted by another officer to what I would describe as the quartermaster's stores. There I am handed one towel (green), one toothbrush (red), one tube of toothpaste, one comb, two Bic razors and one plastic plate, plastic bowl and plastic cutlery.

Having placed my new prison property in the plastic bag along with the few possessions I am allowed to retain, I am escorted to the induction wing. Mr Thompson, the induction officer, invites me into his office. He begins by telling me that he has been in the Prison Service for ten years, and therefore hopes he will be able to answer any questions I might have.

'You begin your life on the induction wing,' he explains, 'where you'll share a cell with another prisoner.' My heart sinks as I recall my experience at Belmarsh. I warn him that whoever I

---

* The Baroness Nicholson had written to Scotland Yard asking them to make a full enquiry into what had happened to the £57 million raised for the Kurds by the Simple Truth campaign which I spearheaded in 1991. This resulted in my being moved to a C-cat closed prison from Belmarsh rather than a D-cat open prison as originally planned. She had insinuated that not all the money had reached the Kurds, hinting that some of it may have ended up in my pocket. My D-cat status will be reinstated once the enquiry has been completed. This must be the first example, in British legal history, of someone being presumed guilty, and sentenced, even before being interviewed by the police.

share a cell with will sell his story to the tabloids. Mr Thompson laughs. How quickly will he find out? Prison would be so much more bearable if you could share a cell with someone you know. I can think of a dozen people I'd be happy to share a cell with, and more than a dozen who ought to be in one.

When Mr Thompson finishes his introductory talk, he goes on to assure me that I will be moved into a single cell on another block once I've completed my induction.*

'How long will that take?' I ask.

'We're so overcrowded at the moment,' he admits, 'that it could take anything up to a month.' He pauses. 'But in your case I hope it will be only a few days.'

Mr Thompson then describes a typical day in the life of Wayland, making it clear that prisoners spend considerably less time locked in their cells than they do at Belmarsh, which is a slight relief. He then lists the work choices: education, gardening, kitchen, workshop or wing cleaner. But he warns me that it will take a few days before this can be sorted out. Nothing is ever done today in the Prison Service, and rarely even tomorrow. He describes how the canteen works, and confirms that I will be allowed to spend £12.50 per week there. I pray that the food will be an improvement on Belmarsh. Surely it can't be worse.

Mr Thompson ends his dissertation by telling me that he's selected a quiet room-mate, who shouldn't cause me any trouble. Finally, as I have no more questions, he accompanies me out of his little office down a crowded corridor packed with young men aged between eighteen to twenty-five, who just stand around and stare at me.

---

* There are four main blocks at Wayland – A, B, C, D. The induction wing is part of A block. There is also a separate block, E. However, this is designated for sex offenders only, and is at the far end of the prison on the other side of a high wire fence.

My heart sinks when he unlocks the door. The cell is filthy and would have been the subject of a court order by the RSPCA if any animal had been discovered locked inside. The window and window sill are caked in thick dirt – not dust, months of accumulated dirt – the lavatory and the wash basin are covered not with dirt, but shit. I need to get out of here as quickly as possible. It is clear that Mr Thompson doesn't see the dirt and is oblivious to the cell's filthy condition. He leaves me alone only for a few moments before my cell-mate strolls in. He tells me his name, but his Yorkshire accent is so broad that I can't make it out and resort to checking on the cell card attached to the door.

Chris* is about my height but more stocky. He goes on talking at me, but I can understand only about one word in three. When he finally stops talking he settles down on the top bunk to read a letter from his mother while I begin to make up my bed on the bunk below. He chuckles and reads out a sentence from her letter: 'If you don't get this letter, let me know and I'll send you another one.' By the time we are let out to collect our supper I have discovered that he is serving a five-year sentence for GBH (grievous bodily harm), having stabbed his victim with a Stanley knife. This is Mr Thompson's idea of someone who isn't going to cause me any trouble.

6.00 pm

All meals are served at a hotplate, situated on the floor below. I wait patiently in a long queue only to discover that the food is every bit as bad as Belmarsh. I return to my cell empty-handed,

---

* Where prisoners have requested not to have their real names included, I have respected their wishes.

grateful that canteen orders at Wayland are on a Friday (tomorrow). I extract a box of Sugar Puffs from my plastic bag and fill the bowl, adding long-life milk. I munch a Belmarsh apple and silently thank Del Boy.*

6.30 pm

Exercise: there are several differences between Belmarsh and Wayland that are immediately apparent when you walk out into the exercise yard. First, you are not searched, second, the distance you can cover without retracing your steps can be multiplied by five – about a quarter of a mile – third, the ratio of black to white prisoners is now 30/70 – compared to 70/30 at Belmarsh – and fourth, my arrival in Norfolk causes even more unsolicited pointing, sniggering and loutish remarks, which only force me to curtail my walk fifteen minutes early. I wish Mr Justice Potts could experience this for just one day.

On the first long circuit, the salesmen move in.

'Anything you need, Jeff? Drugs, tobacco, phonecards?'

They're all quite happy to receive payment on the outside by cheque or cash.† I explain to them all firmly that I'm not interested, but it's clearly going to take a few days before they realize I mean it.

When the barrow boys and second-hand salesmen have departed empty-handed, I'm joined by a lifer who tells me he's also sixty-one, but the difference is that he's already served twenty-seven years in prison and still doesn't know when, if ever,

---

* See *Volume One – Belmarsh: Hell*.
† Dealers inside a prison will nominate someone 'on the out' to whom you can send a cheque if you want a regular supply, assuming a) you have the money, b) someone outside is willing to join in this subterfuge. 90 per cent of such transactions are for drugs. But more of that later.

he'll be released. When I ask him what he's in for, he admits to killing a policeman. I begin a conversation with a black man on the other side of me, and the lifer melts away.

Several of the more mature prisoners turn out to be in for 'white collar' crimes: fiddling the DSS, the DTI or HM Customs. One of them, David, joins me and immediately tells me that he's serving five years.

'What for?' I ask.

'Smuggling.'

'Drugs?'

'No, spirits,' he confesses.

'I didn't realize that was against the law. I thought you could pop across to Calais and . . .'

'Yeah, you can, but not sixty-five times in sixty-five days with a two-ton lorry, carrying twenty million quid's worth of whisky.' He pauses. 'It's when you forget to cough up eight million quid in duty that the Customs and Excise become a little upset.'

A young man in his late twenties takes the place of the police murderer on the other side of me. He brags that he's been banged up in six jails during the past ten years, so if I need a Cook's tour he's the best-qualified operator.

'Why have you been sent to six jails in ten years?' I enquire.

'No one wants me,' he admits. 'I've done over two thousand burglaries since the age of nineteen, and every time they let me out, I just start up again.'

'Isn't it time to give it up, and find something more worthwhile to do?' I ask naively.

'No chance,' he replies. 'Not while I'm making over two hundred grand a year, Jeff.'

After a time, I become sick of the catcalling, so leave the exercise yard and return to my cell, more and more disillusioned, more and more cynical. I don't consider young people, who are first offenders and have been charged with minor offences, should be sent to establishments like this, where one in three will end up on drugs, and one in three will commit a far more serious offence once they've received tuition from the prison professors.

The next humiliation I have to endure is prisoners queuing up silently outside my cell door to get a look at me. No 'Hi, Jeff, how are you?' Just staring and pointing, as if I'm some kind of an animal at the zoo. I sit in my cage, relieved when at eight o'clock an officer slams the doors closed.

8.00 pm

I'm just about to start writing up what has happened to me today when Chris switches on the television. First we have half an hour of *EastEnders* followed by *Top Gear*, and then a documentary on Robbie Williams. Chris is clearly establishing his right to leave the TV on, with a programme he has selected, at a volume that suits him. Will he allow me to watch *Frasier* tomorrow?

I lie in bed on my thin mattress, my head resting on a rock-hard pillow, and think about Mary and the boys, aware that they too must be enduring their own private hell. I feel as low as I did during my first night at Belmarsh. I have no idea what time I finally fall asleep. I thought I had escaped from hell.

So much for purgatory.

DAY 23   FRIDAY 10 AUGUST 2001

5.49 am

Intermittent, fitful sleep, unaided by a rock-hard pillow, a cell-mate who snores and occasionally talks in his sleep; sadly, nothing of literary interest. Rise and write for two hours.

7.33 am

Cell-mate wakes and grunts. I carry on writing. He then jumps off the top bunk and goes to the lavatory in the corner of the cell. He has no inhibitions in front of me, but then he has been in prison for five years. I am determined never to go to the loo in my cell, while I'm still in a one-up, one-down, unless he is out.* I go on working as if nothing is happening. It's quite hard to distract me when I'm writing, but when I look up I see Chris standing there in the nude. His chest is almost completely covered with a tattoo of an eagle towering over a snake, which he tells me with pride he did himself with a tattoo gun. On the

---

* For hygiene reasons it's now against European law to have a lavatory in the cell, especially if it's also your eating place. The British ignore this rule, preferring to pay a heavy fine each year. There are several such rules the Prison Service ignores with impunity.

knuckles of his fingers on both hands are diamonds, hearts, spades and clubs, while on his shoulders he has a massive spider's web that creeps down his back. There's not much pink flesh left unmarked. He's a walking canvas.

8.00 am

The cell doors are unlocked so we can all go and have breakfast; one hour earlier than in Belmarsh. Chris and I walk down to the hotplate. At least the eggs have been boiled quite recently – like today. We're also given a half carton of semi-skimmed milk, which means that I can drop the long-life version from my weekly shopping list and spend the extra 79p on some other luxury, like marmalade.

9.40 am

Mr Newport pops his head round the cell door to announce that Mr Tinkler, the principal officer, would like a word with me. Even the language at Wayland is more conciliatory. When I leave my cell, he adds, 'It's down the corridor, second door on the left.'

When I enter Mr Tinkler's room, he stands up and ushers me into a chair on the other side of his desk as if he were my bank manager. His name is printed in silver letters on a triangular piece of wood, in case anyone should forget. Mr Tinkler resembles an old sea captain rather than a prison officer. He has weathered, lined skin and a neatly cut white beard. He's been in the service for over twenty years and I learn that he will be retiring next August. He asks me how I'm settling in – the most common question asked by an officer when meeting a prisoner for the first time. I tell him about the state of my room and the proclivities of my cell-mate. He listens attentively and, as there is little difference in our age, I detect some sympathy for my predicament. He tells me that as soon as my induction is over he plans to transfer me to a single cell on C block which houses mainly lifers. Mr Tinkler believes that I'll find the atmosphere there more settled, as I will be among a group of prisoners closer to my own age. I leave his office feeling considerably better than when I entered it.

10.01 am

I've only been back in my cell for a few minutes when Mr Newport pops his head round the door again. 'We're moving you to a cell down the corridor. Pack your belongings and follow me.' I hadn't really unpacked so this exercise doesn't take too long. The other cell also turns out to be a double, but once I'm inside Mr Newport whispers, 'We're hoping to leave you on your own.' Mr Tinkler's sympathy is translated into something far more tangible than mere words.

I slowly unpack my possessions from the regulation prison plastic bag for the seventh time in three weeks.

As I now have *two* small cupboards, I put all the prison clothes like shirts, socks, pants, gym kit, etc. in one, while I place my personal belongings in the other. I almost enjoy how long it takes to put my new home in order.

11.36 am

Mr Newport is back again. He's making his rounds, this time to deliver canteen lists to every cell. He has already warned me that if the computer hasn't transferred my surplus cash from Belmarsh I will be allowed an advance of only £5 this week. I quickly check the top of the list, to discover I'm in credit for

£20.46. This turns out to be my weekly allowance of £12.50 plus two payments from the education department at Belmarsh for my lecture on creative writing and two sessions at the workshop. I spend the next thirty minutes planning how to spend this windfall. I allow myself such luxuries as Gillette shaving foam, Robertson's marmalade and four bottles of Evian water.

12 noon

Lunch. On Fridays at Wayland lunch comes in a plastic bag: a packet of crisps, a bar of chocolate, a bread roll accompanied by a lettuce leaf and a sachet of salad cream. I can only wonder in which prison workshop and how long ago this meal was packed, because there are rarely sell-by dates on prison food. I return to my cell to find the canteen provisions have been deposited on the end of my bed in yet another plastic bag. I celebrate by thumbing my bread roll in half and spreading Robertson's Golden Shred all over it with the aid of my tooth-brush handle. I pour myself a mug of Evian. Already the world is a better place.

12.40 pm

Part of the induction process is a private session with the prison chaplain. Mr John Framlington looks to me as if it's been some years since he's administered his own parish. He explains that he's a 'fill-in', as he shares the work with a younger man. I assure him that I will be attending the service on Sunday, but would like to know if it clashes with the RCs. He looks puzzled.

'No, we both use the same chapel. Father Christopher has so many parishes outside the prison to cover each Sunday he holds his service on a Saturday morning at ten thirty.' Mr Framlington is interested to discover why I wish to attend both services. I tell him about my daily diary, and my failure to hear Father Kevin's sermon while at Belmarsh. He sighs.

'You'll quickly find out that Father Christopher preaches a far better sermon than I do.'

2.40 pm

The first setback of the day. Mr Newport returns, the bearer of bad news. Six new prisoners have arrived this afternoon, and once again I will have to share. I learn later that there are indeed six new inductees but as the prison still has several empty beds there is no real need for me to share. However, there are several reporters hanging around outside the prison gates, so the authorities don't want to leave the press with the impression I might be receiving preferential treatment. Mr Newport claims he has selected a more suitable person to share with me. Perhaps this time it won't be a Stanley-knife stabber, just a machete murderer.

I transfer all my personal possessions out of one of the cupboards and stuff them into the other, along with the prison kit.

3.18 pm

My new room-mate appears carrying his plastic bag. He introduces himself as Jules (see plate section). He's thirty-five and has a five-year sentence for drug dealing. He's already been told that I don't smoke.

I watch him carefully as he starts to unpack, and I begin to relax. He has an unusual number of books, as well as an electric chessboard. I feel confident the evening viewing will not be a rerun of *Top of the Pops* and motorbike scrambling. At five to four I leave him to continue his unpacking while I make my way to the gym for another induction session.

3.55 pm

Twenty new inmates are escorted to the gym. There are no doors to be unlocked on our unimpeded journey to the other side of the building. I also notice that on the way we pass a library. I never even found the library at Belmarsh.

The gym is an even bigger shock. It's quite magnificent. Wayland has a full-size basketball court, which is fully equipped for badminton and tennis. The gym instructor asks us to take a seat on a bench where we're handed forms to fill in, giving such details as age, weight, height and sports we are interested in.

'My name is John Maiden,' he tells us, 'and I'm happy to be called John.' I never learnt the first name of any officer at Belmarsh. He tells us the different activities available: cricket, basketball, badminton, football, rugby and, inevitably, weight training. He then takes us into the next room, an area over-crowded with bars, dumb-bells and weights. Once again I'm disappointed to discover that there is only one treadmill, three rowing machines and no step machine. However, there are some very strange-looking bikes, the likes of which I've never seen before.

A gym orderly (a prisoner who has obviously been trained by Mr Maiden) takes us round the room and describes how to use each piece of equipment. He carries out the task most professionally, and should have no trouble finding a job once he leaves prison. I'm listening intently about bench pressing when I find Mr Maiden standing by my side.

'Are you still refereeing rugby?' he asks.

'No. I gave up about ten years ago,' I tell him. 'Once the laws started to change every season I just couldn't keep up. In any case I found that even if I only refereed veteran teams I couldn't keep up, quite literally.'

'Don't let knowledge of the laws worry you,' said Mr Maiden, 'we'll still be able to use you.'

The session ends with a look at the changing room, the shower facilities and, more importantly, clean lavatories. I'm issued with a plastic gym card and look forward to returning to my old training regime.

5.00 pm

Back in the cell, I find Jules sitting on the top bunk reading. I settle down to another session of writing before we're called for supper.

6.00 pm

I select the vegetarian pie and chips and am handed the obligatory yellow lollipop, which is identical to those we were given at Belmarsh. If it's the same company who makes and supplies them to every one of Her Majesty's prisons, that must be a contract worth having. Although it's only my third meal since I arrived, I think I've already spotted the power behind the hotplate. He's a man of about thirty-five, six foot three and must weigh around twenty-seven stone. As I pass him I ask if we could meet later. He nods in the manner of a man who knows that in the kingdom of the blind ... I can only hope that I've located Wayland's 'Del Boy'.

After supper we are allowed to be out of our cells for a couple of hours (Association) until we're banged up at eight.

What a contrast to Belmarsh. I use the time to roam around the corridors and familiarize myself with the layout. The main office is on the first landing and is the hub of the whole wing. From there everything is an offshoot. I also check where all the phones are situated, and when a prisoner comes off one he warns me, 'Never use the phone on the induction landing, Jeff, because the conversations are taped. Use this one. It's a screw-free line.'

I thank him and call Mary in Cambridge. She's relieved that I've rung as she has no way of contacting me, and can't come to see me until she's been sent a visiting order. I promise to put one in tomorrow's post, and then she may even be able to drive across next Tuesday or Wednesday. I remind her to bring some form of identification and that she mustn't try to pass anything over to me, not even a letter.

Mary then tells me that she's accepted an invitation to go on the *Today* programme with John Humphrys. She intends to ask Baroness Nicholson to withdraw her accusation that I stole money from the Kurds, so that I can be reinstated as a D-cat prisoner and quickly transferred to an open prison. I tell Mary that I consider this an unlikely scenario.

'She's not decent enough to consider such a Christian act,' I warn my wife.

'I'm sure you're right,' Mary replies, 'but I will be able to refer to Lynda Chalker's parliamentary reply on the subject and ask why Ms Nicholson wasn't in the House that day if she cares so much about the Kurds, or why had she not at least read the report in Hansard the following morning.' Mary adds that the BBC have told her that they accept I have no case to answer.

'When are you going on?'

'Next Wednesday or Thursday, so it's important I see you before then.'

I quickly agree as my units are running out. I then ask Mary to warn James that I'll phone him at the office at eleven tomorrow morning, and will call her again on Sunday evening. My units are now down to ten so I say a quick goodbye.*

I continue my exploration of the wing and discover that the main Association room and the servery/hotplate double up. The room is about thirty paces by twenty and has a full-size snooker table which is so popular that you have to book a week in advance. There is also a pool table and a table-tennis table, but no TV, as it would be redundant when there's one in every cell.

I'm walking back upstairs when I bump into the hotplate man. He introduces himself as Dale† and invites me to join him in his cell, telling me on the way that he's serving eight years for wounding with intent to endanger life. He leads me down a flight of stone steps onto the lower-ground floor. This is an area I would never have come across, as it's reserved for enhanced prisoners only – the chosen few who have proper jobs and are considered by the officers to be trustworthy. As you can't be granted enhanced status for at least three months, I will never enjoy such luxury, as I am hoping to be moved to a D-cat fairly quickly.

Although Dale's cell is exactly the same size as mine, there the similarity ends. His brick walls are in two tones of blue, and he has nine five-by-five-inch steel mirrors over his washbasin shaped in a large triangle. In our cell, Jules and I have one mirror between us. Dale also has two pillows, both soft, and an extra blanket. On the wall are photos of his twin sons, but no sign of a wife – just the centrefold of a couple of Chinese girls, Blu-tacked

---

* Each week you can buy two £2 phonecards comprising twenty units each. Each card lasts for about twenty minutes so I have to ration myself. Mary, James, William, Alison (my PA), my solicitor and, if there are any units over, friends. You quickly learn not to chatter.
† Also known as Big Mac.

above his bed. He pours me a Coca-Cola, my first since William and James visited me in Belmarsh, and asks if he can help in any way.

'In every way, I suspect. I would like a soft pillow, a fresh towel every day and my washing taken care of.'

'No problem,' he says, like a banker who can make an electronic transfer of a million dollars to New York by simply pressing a button – as long as you *have* a million dollars.

'Anything else? Phonecards, food, drink?'

'I could do with some more phonecards and several items from the canteen.'

'I can also solve that problem,' Dale says. 'Just write out a list of what you want and I'll have everything delivered to your cell.'

'But how do I pay you?'

'That's the easy part. Send in a postal order and ask for the money to be placed against my account. Just make sure the name Archer isn't involved, otherwise there's bound to be an investigation. I won't charge you double-bubble, just bubble and a half.'*

Three or four other prisoners stroll into Dale's cell, so he immediately changes the subject. Within minutes the atmosphere feels more like a club than a prison, as they all seem so relaxed in each other's company. Jimmy, who's serving a three-and-a-half year sentence for being an Ecstasy courier (carrying packages from one club to another), wants to know if I play cricket.

'The occasional charity match, about twice a year,' I admit.

'Good, then you'll be batting number three next week, against D wing.'

---

* Double-bubble: meaning certain debts have to be repaid twice over. This is an understood rule amongst prisoners.

'But I usually go in at number eleven,' I protest, 'and have been known to bat as high as number ten.'

'Then you'll be first wicket down at Wayland,' says Jimmy. 'By the way, we haven't won a match this year. Our two best batsmen got their D-cats at the beginning of the season and were transferred to Latchmere House in Richmond.'

After about an hour of their company, I become aware of the other big difference on the enhanced wing – the noise, or rather the lack of noise. You just don't hear the incessant stereos attempting to out-blare each other.

At five to eight I make my way back to my cell and am met on the stairs by an officer who tells me that I cannot visit the enhanced area again as it's off limits. 'And if you do, Archer,' he adds, 'I'll put you on report, which could mean a fortnight being added to your sentence.'

There's always someone who feels he has to prove how powerful he is, especially if he can show off in front of other prisoners – 'I put Archer in his place, didn't I?' In Belmarsh it was the young officer with his record bookings. I have a feeling I've just met Wayland's.

Back in my cell, I find Jules is playing chess against a phantom opponent on his electronic board. I settle down to write an account of the day. There are no letters to read as no one has yet discovered I'm in Wayland.

8.15 pm

Dale arrives with a soft pillow and an extra blanket. He's disappeared before I can thank him.

DAY 24   SATURDAY 11 AUGUST 2001

5.07 am

I've managed to sleep for six hours, thanks to Jules hanging a blanket from the top bunk, so that it keeps out the fluorescent arc lights that glare through the bars all night.* At 5.40 I place my feet on the linoleum floor and wait. Jules doesn't stir. So far no snoring or talking in his sleep. Last night Jules made an interesting observation about sleep: it's the only time when you're not in jail, and it cuts your sentence by a third. Is this the reason why so many prisoners spend so much time in bed? Dale adds that some of them are 'gouching out' after chasing the dragon. This can cause them to sleep for twelve to fourteen hours, and helps kill the weekend, as well as themselves.

8.15 am

The cell door is unlocked just as I'm coming to the end of my first writing session. During that time I've managed a little over two thousand words.

I go downstairs to the hotplate hoping to pick up a carton of milk, only to be told by Dale that it's not available at the weekend.

---

* The lights are on all night to make sure you don't even think about escaping.

9.00 am

I'm first in the queue at the office, to pick up a VO for Mary. In a C-cat you're allowed one visit every two weeks. A prisoner can invite up to three adults and two children under the age of sixteen. The majority of prisoners are between the ages of nineteen and thirty, so a wife or partner plus a couple of young children would be the norm. As my children are twenty-nine and twenty-seven, it will be only Mary and the boys who I'll be seeing regularly.

10.00 am

I attend my first gym session. Each wing is allowed to send twenty inmates, so after my inability to get on the list at Belmarsh, I make sure that I'm at the starting gate on time.

The main gym is taken up with four badminton matches – like snooker it's a sport that is so popular in prison that you have to book a court a week in advance. The weight-training room next door is packed with heaving and pumping musclemen, and by the time I arrive, someone is already jogging on the one treadmill. I begin my programme with some light stretching before going on the rowing machine. I manage only 1,800 metres in ten minutes, compared with the usual 2,000 I do back in the gym on Albert Embankment. But at least that leaves me something to aim for. I manage a little light weight training before the running machine becomes free. I start at five miles an hour for six minutes to warm up, before moving up to eight miles an hour for another ten minutes. Just to give you an idea how feeble this is, Roger Bannister's four-minute mile in 1952 was at fifteen miles an hour, and I once saw Seb Coe do twelve miles an hour for ten minutes – hold your breath – at the age of forty.

And he was only warming up for a judo session. I end with ten minutes of stretching and a gentle warm down. Most of the prisoners walk into the gym and go straight on to the heavy weights without bothering to warm up. Later they wonder why they pull muscles and are then out of action for the next couple of weeks.

I return to my cell and try out the shower on our wing. The wash room has four showers which produce twice as many jets of water as those at Belmarsh. Also, when you press the button the water continues to flow for at least thirty seconds before you have to press it again. There are two young black lads already showering who, I notice, keep their boxer shorts on (I later learn this is because they're Muslims). However, one problem I still encounter is that I'm allowed only two small, thin towels (three by one foot) a week. If I intend to go to the gym five days a week, followed by a shower ... I'll have to speak to Dale about the problem.

11.30 am

I give James a call at the flat and ask him to send £100 in postal orders to Dale at Wayland so I can buy a razor, some shampoo, a dozen phonecards as well as some extra provisions. I also ask him to phone Griston Post Office and order *The Times* and *Telegraph* every day, Sundays included. James says he'll ask Alison to call them on Monday morning, because he's going on holiday and will be away for a couple of weeks. I'll miss him, even on the phone, and it won't be that long before Will has to return to America.

12.00 noon

I skip lunch because I need to start the second draft of today's script, and in any case, it looks quite inedible. I open a packet of crisps and bite into an apple while I continue writing.

2.00 pm

When the cell door is unlocked again at two o'clock, Dale is standing outside and says he's been given clearance to invite me down to the enhancement wing. The officer I bumped into yesterday must be off duty.

It's like entering a different world. We go straight to Dale's cell, and the first thing he asks me is if I play backgammon. He produces a magnificent leather board with large ivory counters. While I'm considering what to do with a six and a three, never a good opening throw, he points to a plastic bag under the bed. I look inside: a Gillette Mach3 razor, two packets of blades, a bar of Cusson's soap, some shaving foam, a bunch of bananas, a packet of cornflakes and five phonecards. I think it unwise to ask any questions. I thank Dale and hand him my next shopping list. I assure him funds are on the way. We shake hands on a bubble and a half. He'll supply whatever I need from the canteen and charge me an extra 50 per cent. The alternative is to be starved, unshaven or cut to ribbons by a prison razor. This service will also include extra towels, my laundry washed every Thursday, plus a soft pillow, all at an overall expense of around £30 a week.

We are once again joined by two other inmates, Darren (see plate section) and Jimmy (transporting Ecstasy). During the afternoon I play both of them at backgammon, win one and lose one, which seems acceptable to everyone present. Dale leaves us to

23

check in for work as No. 1 on the hotplate, so we all move across to Darren's cell. During a game of backgammon I learn that Darren was caught selling cannabis, a part-time occupation, supplementing his regular job as a construction contractor. I ask him what he plans to do once he leaves prison in a year's time having completed three years of a six-year sentence. He admits he's not sure. I suspect, like so many inmates who can make fifty to a hundred thousand pounds a year selling drugs, he'll find it difficult to settle for a nine to five job.

Whenever he's contemplating his next move, I try to take in the surroundings. You can learn so much about a person from their cell. On the shelves are copies of the *Oxford Shorter Dictionary* (two volumes), the *Oxford Book of Quotations* (he tells me he tries to learn one a day) and a dozen novels that are clearly not on loan from the library. As the game progresses, he asks me if Rupert Brooke owned the Old Vicarage, or just lived there. I tell him that the great war poet only resided there while working on his fellowship dissertation at King's College.*

Jimmy tells me that they're plotting to have me moved down to the enhanced wing as soon as I've completed my induction. This is the best news I've had since arriving at Wayland. The cell door swings open, and Mr Thompson looks round.

'Ah,' he says, when he spots me. 'The governor wants a word.'†

I accompany Mr Thompson to Mr Carlton-Boyce's office.

---

* Brooke wrote to his mother begging her to buy the house while he was training at Betteshanger in the early days of the war. She did so, but not until after he'd died on a troop ship off the Greek coast in 1915. He is buried on the island of Skyros.

† The expression 'governor' does not mean that he or she is the senior officer in the prison. Most prisons have between three and five governors, in charge of different departments. The head of the prison is known as the No. 1 governor or the governing governor.

He's a man of about forty, perhaps forty-five. He welcomes me with a warm smile, and introduces me to the senior officer from C wing, which, he tells me, is where they plan to transfer me. I ask if they would consider me for the enhancement spur, but am told the decision has already been made. I've come to realize that once the machine has decided on something, it would be easier to turn the QEII around than try to get them to change their collective minds.

Mr Carlton-Boyce explains that he would quite happily move me to C wing today, but with so many press sniffing around outside, it mustn't look as if I am being given special treatment, so I have to be the last of my intake to be moved. No need to explain to him the problem of rap music and young prisoners hollering from window to window* all night, but, he repeats, the press interest is tying his hands.

4.00 pm

I return to my cell and continue writing. I've only managed a few pages when I'm interrupted by a knock on the cell door. It's a young man from across the corridor who looks to be in his early twenties.

'Can you write a letter for me?' he asks. No one ever introduces themselves or bothers with pleasantries.

'Yes, of course. Who is it to, and what do you want me to say?' I reply, turning to a blank page on my pad.

'I want to be moved to another prison,' he tells me.

'Don't we all?'

'What?'

'No, nothing, but why should they consider moving you?'

---

* Known as window warriors.

'I want to be nearer my mother, who's suffering from depression.' I nod. He tells me his name is Naz, and then gives me the name of the officer to whom he wishes to address the letter. He asks me to include the reason his request should be taken seriously. I pen the letter, reading each sentence out as I complete it. He signs along the bottom with a flourish. I can't read his signature, so I ask him to spell his name so I can print it in capitals underneath – then the officer in question will know who it's come from, I explain. I place the missive in an envelope, address it, and he seals it. Naz picks up the envelope, smiles and says, 'Thank you. If you want anything, just let me know.' I tell him I need a pair of flip-flops for the shower because I'm worried about catching verrucas. He looks anxiously at me.

'I was only joking,' I say, and wish him luck.

5.00 pm

Supper. I settle for a lump of cabbage and half a portion of chips, which is a normal portion in your world. The cabbage is floating around in water and reminds me of school meals, and why I never liked the vegetable in the first place. While I'm waiting in line, Jimmy tells me that he didn't enjoy his spell of serving behind the hotplate.

'Why not?' I ask.

'The inmates never stop complaining,' he adds.

'About the quality of the food?'

'No, about not giving them large enough portions, especially when it comes to chips.'

When I return to the cell, I find over a hundred letters stacked on the end of my bunk. Jules reminds me that at weekends we're banged up at around five thirty and will remain locked in our cells until eight fifteen the following morning. So

I'll certainly have enough time to read every one of them. Fourteen hours of incarceration, once again blamed on staff shortages. Unpleasant, but still a great improvement on Belmarsh. I say unpleasant only because when you've finished your meal, you're left with dirty, smelly plastic plates littering your tiny cell all night. It might be more sensible to leave the cell doors open for another twenty minutes so that prisoners can scrape the remains of their food into the dustbins at the end of each corridor and then wash their utensils in the sink. And don't forget that in many prisons there are three inmates to a cell with one lavatory.

I compromise, scrape my food into a plastic bag and then tie it up before dropping it in the waste-paper bin next to the lavatory. When I look out of my cell window I notice several prisoners are throwing the remains of their meal through the bars and out onto the grass.

Jules tells me that he's working on a letter to the principal officer (Mr Tinkler) about having his status changed from C-cat to D-cat. He asks if I will go through it with him. I don't tell him that I'm facing the same problem.

Jules is a model prisoner and deserves his enhanced status. He gained this while he was at Bedford where he became a Listener.* He's also quiet and considerate about my writing regime. He so obviously regrets his involvement with drugs, and is one of the few prisoners I've come across who I am convinced will never see the inside of a jail again. I do a small editorial job on his letter and suggest that we should go over the final draft tomorrow. I then spend the next couple of hours reading

---

* Selected prisoners are invited to become Listeners. They are trained by the Samaritans so that they can assist fellow inmates who are facing problems, some so depressed they even contemplate suicide.

through today's mail, which is just as supportive as the letters I received in Belmarsh. There is, however, one missive of a different nature that I feel I ought to share with you.

> *University College Hospital*
> *London 1/8/01 4.30 pm*

My dear Lord Archer

Many poets and writers have written much of their best work in prison, OW for one. However, I cannot conceive of you having to spend four miserable years in a maximum security prison. I spent 60 days in such a facility in Canada on a trumped-up charge of disturbing the peace.

I escaped by a most devious means.

I can arrange for your immediate release from bondage, however, only if you are willing to donate £15m to my charity foundation.

I can be contacted anytime at 020 7— If you would like some company, choose three non-criminal or white-collar offenders to join with you, for an appropriate amount.

Yours as an artist,

I am quite unable to read the signature. In the second post there is another letter in the same bold red hand:

> *1/8/01 5.05 pm*

Dear Geofrey [sic]

After having sealed the letter to you I realized that I wrote £15m instead of £1.5m So just to reassure you, I'm not an idiot, I repeat my offer to spring you and a few other trustworthy buddies!

Yours in every greater art,

Again, I cannot read the signature.

DAY 25   SUNDAY 12 AUGUST 2001

5.56 am

Woken by voices in the corridor, two officers, one of them on a walkie-talkie. They open a cell door and take a prisoner away. I will find out the details when my door is unlocked in a couple of hours' time.

6.05 am

Write for two hours.

8.15 am

Breakfast. Sugar Puffs (prison issue), long-life milk (mine, because it's Sunday). Beans on burnt toast (prison's).

10.00 am

I go to the library for the first time and sign up. You are allowed to take out two books, a third if your official work is education. The library is about the same size as the weight-lifting room and, to be fair, just as well stocked. They have everything from Graham Greene to Stephen King, *I, Claudius* to Harry Potter.

However, although Forsyth, Grisham, Follett and Jilly Cooper are much in evidence, I can find none of my books on the shelves. I hope that's because they are all out on loan. Lifers often tell me they've read them all – slowly – and in some cases several times.

I take out a copy of *The Glass Bead Game* by Hermann Hesse, which I haven't read in years, and *Famous Trials* selected by John Mortimer. Naturally I have to fill in another form, and then my choices are stamped by the library orderly – a prisoner – to be returned by 26 August. I'm rather hoping to have moved on by then.

Kevin, the prisoner who stamps my library card, tells me that all my books were removed from the shelves the day they found out I was being transferred to Wayland.

'Why?' I ask.

'Direct order from the number one governor. It seems that Belmarsh informed her that the prisoners were stealing your books, and if they could then get you to sign them, the black-market price is a thousand pounds.'

I believe everything except the thousand pounds, which sounds like a tabloid figure.

10.30 am

I check my watch, leave the library and quickly make my way across to the chapel on the other side of the corridor. There is no officer standing by the entrance. It suddenly hits me that I haven't been searched since the day I arrived. I'm a couple of minutes late, and wonder if I've come to the wrong place, as there are only three other prisoners sitting in the pews, along with the chaplain. John Framlington is dressed in a long, black gown and black cape with crimson piping, and welcomes me with literally open arms.

The chapel is very impressive, with its wood-panelled walls and small oils depicting the life of Christ. The simple altar is covered in a cloth displaying a white cross with splashes of gold. There is also a large wooden cross hanging from the wall behind the altar. The seating consists of six rows of twenty wooden chairs set in a semicircle reminiscent of a small amphitheatre. I take a seat in the third row as a group of men and women all dressed in red T-shirts enters by the backdoor. They assemble their music on stands while a couple strap on guitars and a flautist practises a few notes. She's very pretty. I wonder if it's because it's my twenty-fifth day in prison. But that would be an ungallant thought. She is pretty.

By ten forty-five the congregation has swelled to seven, but we are still outnumbered by the nine-strong choir. The prisoners are all seated to the right of the altar while the choir is standing on the left. A man, who appears to be the group's leader, suggests we move across and join him on their side of the chapel. All seven of us dutifully obey. I've just worked out why the congregation at Belmarsh was over two hundred, week in and week out, while at Wayland it's down to seven. Here you are allowed to stroll around the buildings for long periods of time, so if you wish to make contact with someone from another wing, it's not all that difficult. In Belmarsh, chapel was a rare opportunity to catch up with a friend from another block, relay messages, pass on drugs and occasionally even pray.

The chaplain then walks up to the front, turns and welcomes us all. He begins by introducing Shine who, he tells us, are a local group that perform for several churches in the diocese.

We all join in the first hymn, 'He Who Would Valiant Be', and Shine turn out to be rather good. Despite our depleted numbers, the service still swings along. Once the chaplain has delivered the opening prayer, he comes and sits amongst the congregation. He doesn't conduct any other part of the service, as that has been left in the capable hands of the leader of Shine. Next we sing 'Amazing Grace', which is followed by a lesson from Luke, read by another member of the group. Following another hymn we are addressed by the leader of Shine. He takes his text from the first reading of the Good Samaritan. He talks about people who walk by on the other side when you are in any trouble. This time I do thank God for my family and friends, because so few of them have walked by on the other side.

The service ends with a blessing from the chaplain, who then thanks the group for giving up their time. I return to my cell and write notes on everything I have just experienced.

12.09 pm

I call Mary in Grantchester. How I miss my weekends with her, strolling around the garden at the Old Vicarage: the smell of the flowers and the grass, feeding the fish and watching students idly punting on the Cam. Mary briefs me on what line she intends to take on the *Today* programme, now that the Foreign Office and the KDP (Kurdish Democratic Party) have confirmed how the money for the Kurds was raised and distributed. I try to think how Ms Nicholson will spin herself out of this one.

Mary reminds me that she can't come to see me until she receives a VO. I confirm I sent her one yesterday. She goes on to tell me that her own book, *Photoconversion Volume One: Clean Electricity from Photovoltaics* (advance sales 1,229, price £110), has been well received by the academic world.

We finish by discussing family matters. Although I've come to the end of my twenty units, I don't tell her that I am in possession of another two phonecards as that might cause trouble for Dale, especially if the conversation is being taped. I promise to call her again on Tuesday, and we agree a time. Just in case you've forgotten, the calls are always one way: OUT.

My next call is to James, who is giving a lunch party for ten friends at our apartment in London. I do miss his cooking. He tells me who's sitting round my table and what they are eating: Roquefort, fig and walnut salad, spaghetti, and ice cream, followed by Brie, Stilton or Cheddar. This will be accompanied by an Australian red and a Californian white. I begin to salivate.

'Dinner,'* yells an officer, and I quickly return to the real world.

12.20 pm

Lunch: Chinese stir-fried vegetables (they may have been stirred, but they are still glued together), an apple, supplemented by a Mars bar (30p), and a glass of Evian. Guests: pre-selected.

1.00 pm

I join Dale on the enhanced wing. I grab Darren's *Sunday Times*, and read very slowly while Dale and Jimmy play backgammon. The lead story is the alleged rape of a girl in Essex by Neil and Christine Hamilton. This is more graphically described in Dale's *News of the World*, and the implausible story is memorable for Christine Hamilton's observation, 'If I wanted to do that sort of thing, it would be in Kensington or Chelsea, not Essex.'

We play several games of backgammon, during which time the assembled gathering questions me about the contest for the Tory party leadership. Darren (marijuana only) is a fan of Michael Portillo, and asks how I feel. I tell him that I think it

---

* In prison dinner is lunch, and tea is supper.

might have been wise of the 1922 Committee to let all three candidates who reached the second round – Clarke 59, Duncan Smith 54 and Portillo 53 – be presented to the party membership. Leaving Michael out is bound to create some bad feeling and may even cause trouble in the future. It's quite possible that the membership would have rejected Portillo in any case, but I feel that they should have been allowed the opportunity to do so.

Dale (wounding with intent) is a huge fan of Margaret Thatcher, while Jimmy (Ecstasy courier) voted for John Major. 'A decent bloke,' he says. It's sometimes hard to remember that I may be sitting in a room with an armed robber, a drug dealer, a million-pound fraudster, and heaven only knows who else. It's also worth mentioning that when it comes to their 'other world', they never discuss anything in front of me.

3.00 pm

Exercise: I take the long walk around the perimeter of the prison – about half a mile – and several inmates greet me in a more friendly fashion than they did on my first outing last Thursday. The first person to join me is a man who is obviously on drugs. Unlike William Keane – do you remember him from Belmarsh? – I can't tell which drug he's on just by looking at his skin. His name is Darrell, and he tells me that his original sentence was for ten years. His crime: cutting someone up in a pub with a broken bottle. He was nineteen at the time. I take a second look. He looks about forty.

'Then why are you still here?' I ask, assuming he will explain that he's serving a second or third sentence for another offence.

'Once I ended up in prison, I got hooked on drugs, didn't I?'

'Did you?'

'Yeah, and I'd never taken a drug before I came in. But when you're given a ten-year sentence and then banged up for twenty-two hours a day with prisoners who are already on skag, you sort of fall in with it, don't you? First I was caught smoking cannabis so the governor added twenty-eight days to my sentence.'

'Twenty-eight days for smoking cannabis? But . . .'

'I then tried cocaine and finally moved on to heroin. Every time I got caught, my sentence was lengthened. Mind you, I've been clean for over a year now, Jeff. I've had to be, otherwise I'm never going to get out of this fuckin' shithole, am I?'

'How long has it been?'

'Twenty-one years. I'm forty-one, and over half my sentence has been added because of being caught taking drugs while inside.'

I'm trying to take this in when we're joined by a burly older man of around my height, who looks Middle Eastern. Darrell slips quietly away, which I fear means trouble. The new man doesn't bother with any small talk.

'How would you like to make fifty grand a week while you're still in prison?'

'What do you have in mind?' I ask innocently, because he doesn't look like a publisher.

'I've got a lorry-load of drugs stuck on the Belgian border waiting to come into this country, but I'm a little short of cash at the moment. Put up fifty grand and you'll have a hundred by this time next week.' I quicken my pace and try to lose him, but within seconds he's caught me up. 'There would be no risk for you,' he adds, slightly out of breath. 'We take all the risk. In any case, no one could pin it on you, not while you're still in jail.'

I stop in my tracks and turn to face him. 'I hate drugs, and I detest even more those people who peddle them. If you ever try to speak to me again, I will repeat this conversation, first to my solicitor and then to the governor. And don't imagine you can threaten me, because they would be only too happy to move me out of here, and my bet is your sentence would be doubled. Do I make myself clear?'

I have never seen a more frightened man in my life. What he didn't know was that I was even more terrified than he was. I couldn't forget the punishment meted out in Belmarsh for being a grass – hot water mixed with sugar thrown in your face – or the man with the four razor-blade scars administered in the shower. I quickly leave the exercise yard and go back to my cell, pull the door closed, and sit on the end of the bed, shaking.

4.00 pm

When Jules returns, I'm still shaking. I go off in search of Dale.

'I know that bastard,' says Dale. 'Just leave him to me.'

'What does that mean?' I ask.

'Don't ask.'

'I have to. I'm trying not to cause any trouble.'

'He won't trouble you again, that I guarantee.' He then raises his twenty-seven-stone frame from the end of the bed and departs.

4.30 pm

Association: I emerge from the enhanced wing with two Mars bars, having played a couple of games of backgammon with Darren. I become aware of the most incredible uproar emanating from the games room. Am I about to experience my first riot? I glance anxiously round the door to see a group of West Indians playing dominoes. Every time they place a domino on the table, it's slammed down as if a judge were trying to bring a rowdy courtroom to order. This is followed by screaming delight more normally associated with Lara scoring a century at Sabina Park. The officer on duty, Mr Nutbourne, and the other inmates playing snooker, pool and table tennis don't seem at all disturbed by this. I stroll across to join the dozen or so West Indians and decide to watch a couple of games. One of them looks up from the table, and shouts, 'You wanna try your luck, man?'

'Thank you,' I reply, and take a seat vacated by one of the players.

A West Indian with greying hair divides the dominoes between the four of us and we each end up with seven pieces. The player on my right is able to begin the game as he has a double six. He places his prize with a thump in the middle of the table, which is followed by shouts and screams from the assembled gathering. The game progresses for four rounds without any player failing to place a domino on the end of the line. During the next round the player on my left doesn't have a three or six, so passes and, as I have a six, I place my domino quietly on the table. I notice the brothers are becoming a little less noisy. By this time a large crowd has gathered round until only two of us are left with one domino; I have a five and a four, but it is my opponent's turn. If he's going to win, he has to hit, and hit now. The brothers fall almost silent. Can the player on my left thwart me and win the game? I pray for the second time that day. He has neither a four nor a one, and passes without a murmur. I try desperately to keep a poker face, while holding my last domino in the palm of my hand. A forest of black eyes are staring at me. I quietly place my four next to the four on the right-hand end and so much bedlam breaks out that even Mr Nutbourne decides to find out what's going on. I rise to leave.

'Another game, man? Another game?' they demand.

'How kind of you,' I say, 'but I must get back to my writing. It's been a pleasure to play you.' This is followed by much slapping of hands. I depart quickly, aware that if I were to play a second round, the myth would be shattered. Frankly I know nothing of the subtleties of the game, having just brought a new meaning to the phrase 'beginner's luck'.

5.45 pm

Supper. When I reach the hotplate, Dale takes my plastic bowl and, just as Tony always did at Belmarsh, decides what I shall be allowed to eat. He selects a vegetarian quiche, a few lettuce leaves carefully extracted from a large bowl and a tomato. I will no longer have to think about what to eat as long as Dale's on duty.

6.00 pm

Jules and I are banged up again until eight tomorrow morning. Fourteen hours in a cell seven paces by three, just in case you've forgotten. As it's Sunday, there are no letters awaiting me, so I just go over my script before returning to Hermann Hesse.

9.00 pm

Jules and I watch Meg Ryan and Kevin Kline in *French Kiss*, which has us both laughing, but then we are a captive audience.

10.54 pm

I settle my head on my new soft pillow. It isn't goose down, or even duck feather – just foam rubber – but I know luxury when I feel it.

DAY 26   MONDAY 13 AUGUST 2001

6.03 am

Yesterday's early morning commotion in the corridor turned out to be a prisoner needing medication and the assistance of a Listener. He had pressed the emergency call button. There's one in every cell next to the door which, when pressed, illuminates a small red light in the corridor, while another flashes up in the main office. It is known by the inmates as room service, although prison orders state that it must be used only in emergencies, otherwise you will be placed on report. I couldn't find out why the prisoner needed the help of a Listener, but as it was his first night at Wayland, it could have been for any number of reasons. Remembering my first night, I can only sympathize.

I write for two hours.

8.15 am

Breakfast. Sugar Puffs (mine), milk (theirs). One egg on a slice of toast (theirs), a second slice of toast (theirs), marmalade (mine).

10.00 am

Banged up for two hours, which I plan on using to work on the second draft of this morning's script. That's assuming there are no interruptions – there are two.

10.49 am

The cell door is unlocked by Mr Newport, who wants to talk to Jules about his application for a change of status from C-cat to D-cat. Jules explains that he has written his reasons in a letter so that they (the authorities) will have all the relevant details on record. Mr Newport glances over the two pages and promises to arrange an interview with Mr Stainthorpe, the classifications officer. The cell door is banged shut.

11.09 am

The cell door is opened a second time. On this occasion it's Mr Nutbourne, who says, 'Now tell me, Jeffrey,' (the first officer to call me by my Christian name) 'do you want the good news or the bad news?'

'You decide,' I suggest.

'You won't be going to C wing after all, because we're going to move you down to join your friends on the enhanced corridor.'

'So what's the bad news?' I ask.

'Unfortunately, a cell won't be available until 29 August, when the next prisoner on that corridor will have completed his sentence.'

'But you could still put me in a single cell on another part of the block.'

'Don't push your luck,' he says with a grin, before slamming the door closed.

12 noon

Lunch: soup (minestrone) and a piece of brown bread (fresh). Couldn't face the meat pie. Heaven knows what animal's inside it.

2.00 pm

Gym: I'm the first to set foot in the gym, only to find that the running machine has broken down. Damn, damn, damn.

I warm up and stretch for a few minutes before doing ten minutes on the rower. I manage 1,909 metres, a vast improvement on yesterday. A little light weight training before moving on to a bicycle, the like of which I have never seen before. I can't get the hang of it until Mr Maiden comes to my rescue and explains that once you've set the speed, the peddles just revolve until you stop them. He sets the pace at thirty kilometres per hour, and leaves me to get on with it. I sweat away for ten minutes, and then realize I don't know how to turn it off. I shout to Everett (GBH) for help – a black man who I sat next to during the dominoes encounter – but he just grins, or simply doesn't understand my predicament. When my screaming goes up a decibel, Mr Maiden finally comes to my rescue. He can't stop laughing as he shows me which button I have to press to bring the machine to a halt. It's marked STOP – in red. I fall off the bike, exhausted, which causes much mirth among the other prisoners, especially the dominoes players. I use the rest of my time lying on a rubber mat recovering.

As the prisoners begin to make their way back to their cells – no gates, no searches – I'm called to Mr Maiden's office. Once his door is closed and no other prisoner can overhear, he asks, 'Would you like to join the staff on Friday morning to assist with a special needs group from Dereham Adult Training Centre?'

'Of course I would,' I tell him.

'Jimmy is the only other prisoner who presently helps that group, so perhaps you should have a word with him.'

I thank Mr Maiden and return to my cell. I don't immediately take a shower as I am still sweating from the bicycle experience, so I use the time to call my PA, Alison. I tell her I need more A4 pads and pens because I'm currently writing two to three thousand words a day. I also need stamped envelopes addressed to her – large A4 size for the manuscript and slightly smaller ones so I can turn round my daily postbag.* Alison tells me that because of the sackfuls of letters I am receiving both in prison and at the office, as well as having to type two scripts at once, she's putting in even longer hours than when I was a free man.

'And to think that you were worried about losing your job if I were to end up in jail,' I remind her. 'Just wait until I get my hands back on my novel.† You'll be working weekends as well.'

Alison confirms that the last five chapters of *Belmarsh* have arrived safely, thanks to the cooperation of Roy, the censor. No such problem at Wayland, where you just drop your envelope in a postbox and off it goes. I remind her that I need the *Belmarsh* script back as soon as possible, to go over it once again before I let Jonathan Lloyd (my agent) read it for the first time. My final request is to be put through to Will.

'He's in Cambridge with Mary.'

Although I check to see how many units are left on the phonecard, I haven't needed to worry about the problem lately as Dale seems to be able to arrange an endless supply of them.

---

* You're not allowed stamps as they could be used for trading drugs, but you are permitted stamped addressed envelopes.
† Published in 2002 as *Sons of Fortune*.

I dial Cambridge and catch Mary, who is just leaving to chair a meeting at Addenbrooke's Hospital, where she is deputy chairman. After a few words, she passes me over to Will. He is full of news and tells me Mum has been preparing in her usual diligent way for the *Today* interview. Since he spoke to me last, Andy Bearpark, who covered Kurdish affairs at the Overseas Development Administration during the relevant time, confirms he has been contacted by KPMG regarding the audit. Will feels the police will be left with little choice but to complete their initial report quickly and reinstate my D-cat. I thank him, particularly for the support he's giving his mother. I then tell him that I've finished the Belmarsh section of the diaries and ask if he's found time to read the odd chapter.

'I just can't face it, Dad. It's bad enough that you're there.' I tell him that I have already decided that there will be three volumes of the prison diary: Hell, Purgatory and Heaven, with an epilogue called 'Back to Earth'. This at least makes him laugh. As I'm telling him this, Jimmy passes me in the corridor and I turn to ask if he could spare me a moment. He nods, and waits until I finish my conversation with Will.

Jimmy has also heard that I may be joining them on the enhanced wing, but wonders if Nutbourne's information came from on high.

'Exactly my thoughts,' I tell him. I then mention that Mr Maiden has invited me to join them in the gym on Friday morning to assist with the special needs group. I'm surprised by his reaction.

'You jammy bastard,' says Jimmy. 'I had to wait a couple of years before I was invited to join that shift, and you get asked after four days.' Funnily enough I hadn't thought of it as a perk, but simply as doing something worthwhile.

Jimmy invites me down to his cell for a drink, my only

chance of having a Diet Coke. We're joined by Jason, who spotted me in the corridor. Jason hands me a pair of slippers and a wash bag, which are normally only issued to enhanced prisoners.

'You jammy bastard,' repeats Jimmy, before he starts going on about his weight. Jimmy is six foot one, slim and athletic (see plate section). He trains every day in the gym and is known by the inmates as Brad Pitt.

'More like Arm Pitt,' says Jason.

Jimmy smiles and continues to grumble, 'I need to put on some weight.'

'I like you as you are, darling,' Jason replies.

I decide this is an ideal opportunity to ask them how drugs are smuggled into prison. Both throw out one-liners to my myriad questions, and between them continue my education on the subject.

Of the six major drugs – cannabis, speed, Ecstasy, cocaine, crack cocaine and heroin – only cannabis and heroin are in daily demand in most prisons. Each wing or block has a dealer, who in turn has runners who handle any new prisoners when they arrive on the induction wing. It's known as Drug Induction. This is usually carried out in the yard during the long exercise break each morning. The price ranges from double the street value to as much as a tenfold mark-up depending on supply and demand; even in prison free enterprise prevails. Payment can be made in several ways. The most common currency is phonecards or tobacco. You can also send in cash to be credited to the dealer's account, but most dealers don't care for that route, as even the dumbest officer can work out what they're up to. The preferred method is for the recipient of the drugs to arrange for a friend to send cash to the dealer's contact on the outside, usually his girlfriend, wife or partner. Just as there is a canteen list of prices taped to the wall outside the main office, so there is an accepted but, unprinted list, of available drugs in any prison. For example, the price of five joints of cannabis would work out at around £10 or five phonecards; a short line of cocaine would cost about £10, while heroin, a joey or a bag, which is about half a gram, can cost as much as £20.

Next we discuss the bigger problem of how to get the gear into prison. Jason tells me that there are several ways. The most obvious is via visits, but this is not common as the punishment for being caught usually fits the crime, for both the visitor and the prisoner. If you are caught, you automatically lose your visits and the use of phonecards. For most prisoners this is their only lifeline to the outside world. Few, other than desperate heroin addicts, are willing to sacrifice being able to see their family and friends once a fortnight or speak to them regularly on the phone. So most dealers revert to other safer methods because were they to be caught twice, they not only lose the right to a phonecard as well as a visit, but will be charged with the offence and can expect to have time added to their sentence.

'What are the other methods?' I ask.

'You can arrange to have gear thrown over the wall at a designated time so it can be picked up by a gardener or a litter collector. Helps to supplement their seven pounds a week wages,' Jason explains. 'But home leave or town visits are still the most common source of drugs coming in. A clever courier can earn some extra cash prior to being released.'

'Mind you,' adds Jimmy, 'if you're caught bringing gear in, not only do you lose all your privileges, but you can be transferred to an A-cat with time added to your sentence.'

'What about by post?' I ask.

'Sending in a ballpoint pen is a common method,' Jason says. 'You half fill the tube with heroin and leave the bottom half full of ink, so that when the screws remove the little cap on the bottom they can only see the ink. They could break the tube in half, but that might mean having to replace as many as a hundred biros a week. But the most common approach still involves brown envelopes and underneath stamps.'

'Envelopes?' I ask.

'Down the side of most large brown envelopes is a flap. If you lift it carefully you can place a line of heroin along the inside and carefully seal it back up again. When it comes in the post it looks like junk mail or a circular, but it could be hiding up to a hundred quid's worth of skag.'

'One prisoner went over the top recently,' says Jimmy. 'He'd been enhanced and put on the special wing. One of our privileges is that we can hang curtains in our cell. When his selected curtains arrived, prison staff found the seams were weighed down with heroin. The inmate was immediately locked up in segregation and lost all his privileges.'

'And did he also get time added to his sentence?'

'No,' Jason replies. 'He claimed that the curtains were sent in by his co-defendant from the original trial in an attempt to stitch him up.' I like the use of the words 'stitch him up' in this context. 'Not only did he get away with it,' continues Jimmy, 'but the co-defendant ended up being sentenced to five years. Both men were as guilty as sin, but neither of them ended up in jail for the crime they had committed,' Jimmy adds. Not the first time I've heard that.

'But you can also have your privileges taken away and time added if you're caught *taking* drugs,' Jason reminds me.

'True,' says Jimmy, 'but there are even ways around that. In 1994 the government brought in mandatory drug testing to catch prisoners who were taking illegal substances. But if you're on heroin, all you have to do is purchase a tube of smoker's toothpaste from the canteen and swallow a mouthful soon after you've taken the drug.'

'How does that help?' I ask.

'If they ask for a urine sample,' explains Darren, 'smoker's toothpaste will cloud it, and they have to wait another twenty-four hours before testing you again. By the time they conduct a second test, a couple of gallons of water will have cleared any trace of heroin out of your system. You may be up all night peeing, but you don't lose your privileges or have time added.'*

'But that's not possible with cannabis?' I ask.†

'No, cannabis remains in your bloodstream for at least a month. But it's still big business whatever the risk, and you can be fairly certain that the dealers never touch any drugs themselves. They all have their mules and their sellers. They end up only taking a small cut, and are rarely caught.'

'And some of them even manage to make more money inside prison than they did outside,' adds Jason.

The call for tea is bellowed down the corridor by an officer. I close my notepad, thank Jason for the slippers and wash bag, not to mention the tutorial, and return to my cell.

5.00 pm

Supper: vegetarian pie and two potatoes. If I become enhanced, I will be allowed to have my own plate plus a mug or cup sent in, not to mention curtains.

---

* Providing a contaminated urine sample is a *reportable* charge under prison rules.

† Cannabis can remain in the bloodstream for up to twenty-eight days. On arrival at a remand prison, you can be tested, but are likely to be given twenty-eight days' grace in order to clear your system out. However, if you are found to be positive on the twenty-ninth day, the prison adjudication system comes into force.

6.00 pm

Write for just over an hour.

7.15 pm

Watch Sue Barker and Roger Black sum up the World Athletics Championship, which has been a disaster for Britain. One gold for Jonathan Edwards in the triple jump and a bronze for Dean Macey in the decathlon. The worst result for Britain since the games began in 1983, and that was following such a successful Olympics in Sydney. I'm almost able to convince myself that I'm glad I was prevented from attending.

8.00 pm

Read through my letters. Just over a hundred today.

9.00 pm

Jules and I watch a modern version of *Great Expectations* with Robert De Niro and Gwyneth Paltrow. If I hadn't been in prison, I would have walked out after fifteen minutes.

I begin to read *Famous Trials* selected by John Mortimer. I start with Rattenbury and Stones, the problem of a younger man falling in love with an older woman. Now that's something I haven't experienced. I fall asleep around eleven.

DAY 27   TUESDAY 14 AUGUST 2001

6.18 am

Overslept. After a night's rain, the sun is peeping through my four-bar window. I write for a couple of hours.

8.20 am

Breakfast: two Weetabix, one hard-boiled egg and a piece of toast.

10.56 am

I've been writing for about an hour when the cell door is opened; Mr Clarke tells me that as part of my induction I must attend a meeting with a representative from the BoV (Board of Visitors). Everything has an acronym nowadays.

Nine prisoners assemble in a waiting room opposite Mr Newport's office. There are eleven comfortable chairs set in a semicircle, and a low table in the middle of the room. If there had been a few out-of-date magazines scattered on the table, it could have passed for a GP's waiting room. We have to hang around for a few minutes before being joined by a man in his late fifties, who looks like a retired solicitor or bank manager. He's about five foot nine with greying hair and a warm smile. He wears an open-neck shirt and a pair of grey flannels. I suspect that the only other time he's this casually dressed is on a Sunday afternoon.

He introduces himself as Keith Flintcroft, and goes on to explain that the Board is made up of sixteen local people appointed by the Home Office. They are not paid, which gives them their independence.

'We can see the governor or any officer on request, and although we have no power, we do have considerable influence. Our main purpose,' he continues, 'is to deal with prisoners' complaints. However, our authority ends when it comes to an order of the governor. For example, we cannot stop a prisoner being placed in segregation, but we can make sure that we are supplied with details of the offence within a period of seventy-two hours.* We can also read any written material on a prisoner with the exception of their legal papers or medical records.'

Mr Flintcroft comes over as a thoroughly decent bloke, a man who obviously believes in giving service to the local community. Just like so many thousands of citizens up and down the country he expects little reward other than the satisfaction of doing a worthwhile job. I believe that if he felt a prisoner was getting a rough deal, he would, within the limits of his power, try to do something about it.

He ends his ten-minute chat by saying, 'You'll find that we spend a lot of our time roaming around the prison. You can't miss us because we wear these distinctive buff-coloured name

---

* Often, when a prisoner in segregation asks to see a member of the BoV, that request is not passed on for seventy-two hours, by which time any swelling or wound caused by fighting with an officer will be less obvious.

badges. So feel free to come and talk to us whenever you want to – in complete confidence. Now, are there any questions?'

To my surprise, there are none. Why doesn't anyone mention the state of the cells on the induction wing compared with the rest of the prison? Why, when there is a painter on each wing, who I observe working every day, isn't there one to spruce up the induction wing? Do they leave the wing in a filthy condition so that when inmates are moved to another part of the prison they'll feel it's an improvement, or is it that they just can't cope with the turnover of prisoners? Either way, I would like to tell Governor Kate Cawley (I've discovered the governor's name on a notice board, but haven't yet come across her) that it's degrading, and a blip in an otherwise well-run prison. Why are the induction prisoners locked up for such long hours while the rest of the inmates are given far more freedom? And why ... And then it hits me. I am the only person in that room who hasn't been through this process before, and the others either simply don't give a damn or can't see the point of it. They are mostly hardened criminals who just want to complete their sentence and have as easy a time as possible before returning to a life of crime. They believe that the likes of Mr Flintcroft will make absolutely no difference to their lives. I suspect that the likes of Mr Flintcroft have, over the years, made a great deal of difference to their lives, without their ever realizing or appreciating it.

Once Mr Flintcroft accepts that there are going to be no questions, we all file out and return to our cells. I stop and thank him for carrying out his thankless task.

12 noon

Mr Chapman tells me I have a large parcel in reception, which I can pick up after dinner (lunch).

12.15 pm

Lunch: spam fritters, two potatoes and a glass of Evian. HELP! I'm running out of Evian.

12.35 pm

I report to reception and collect my parcel, or what's left of it. It originally consisted of two books: Alan Clark's *Diaries*, and *The Diving Bell and the Butterfly* by Jean-Dominique Bauby, which has been sent in by Anton, one of James's closest friends. They're accompanied by a long letter about the latest bust-up with his girlfriend (I do love the young – only *their* problems exist) and, from Alison, a dozen writing pads, two packets of liquid-point pens and six books of first-class stamps. Mr Chapman explains that I can keep the long letter from Anton, but everything else will be placed in my box at reception and returned to me only when I'm transferred or released.

3.15 pm

I have become so accustomed to prison life that I not only remember to take my gym card, but also a towel and a bottle of water to my afternoon gym session. The running machine still isn't working, so I'm back to ten minutes on the rower (1,837 metres – not very impressive) followed by a light weight-training session and ten minutes on the bike, which I now know how to turn on and, more importantly, turn off.

Everett (GBH) leaves his 240-pound bench press, and asks if he can have a swig of my Evian. I nod, as I don't think there's much of an alternative. A moment later his black weight-lifting partner – taller and wider – strolls across and takes a swig without asking. By the time I've finished stretching, the bottle is empty.

Once I'm back on my wing I try to take a shower, but the door is locked. I look through the tiny window. It's all steamed up, and two prisoners are banging on the door trying to get out. I cannot believe that it is prison policy to lock them in and me out. I hang around for about ten minutes with a couple of other prisoners before an officer eventually appears. I tell him I'd like to have a shower.

'You've missed your chance.'

'I didn't have a chance,' I tell him. 'It's been locked for the past ten minutes.'

'I've only been away for a minute, maybe two,' he says.

'I've been standing here for nearly ten minutes,' I politely point out.

'If I say it's one minute, it's one minute,' he says.

I return to my cell. I now feel cold and sweaty. I sit down to write.

6.00 pm

Supper. A bowl of thick, oily soup is all I can face. Back in my cell I pour myself half a mug of blackcurrant juice. The only luxury left. At least I'm still losing weight.

6.30 pm

Exercise: I walk around the perimeter fence with Jimmy and Darren. Just their presence stops most inmates from giving me a hard time.

7.00 pm

I finally manage a shower. I then put on a prison tracksuit, grey and baggy, but comfortable. I decide to call Mary. There is a queue for the phone as this is the most popular time of day. When it's my turn, I dial the Old Vicarage only to find that the line is engaged.

I spot Dale hanging around in the corridor, obviously wanting to speak to me. He tells me that the money hasn't arrived. I assure him that if it isn't in the morning post, I'll chase it up. I try Mary again – still engaged. I go back to my cell and prepare my desk for an evening session. I check my watch. It's 7.55 pm. I'll only have one more chance. Back to the phone. I call Cambridge. Still engaged. I return to my cell to find an officer standing by the door. I'm banged up for another twelve hours.

8.00 pm

I read through today's script and then prepare outline notes for the first session tomorrow, to the accompaniment of two West Indians hollering at each other from cells on opposite sides of the wing. I remark to Jules that they seem to be shouting even louder than usual. He resignedly replies that there's not a lot you can do about window warriors. I wonder. Should I push my luck? I go over to the window and suggest in a polite but firm voice that they don't need to shout at each other. A black face appears at the opposite window. I wait for the usual diatribe.

'Sorry, Jeff,' he says, and continues the conversation in a normal voice. Well, you can only ask.

DAY 28   WEDNESDAY 15 AUGUST 2001

6.04 am

I wake, only to remember where I am.

8.15 am

Breakfast: when I go down to the hotplate to collect my meal, Dale gives me a nod to indicate that the money has arrived.

8.30 am

Phone Mary to be told that she's doing the *Today* programme with John Humphrys tomorrow morning and will be visiting me on Friday with Will. As James is on holiday, she suggests that the third place is taken by Jonathan Lloyd. He wants to discuss my new novel, *Sons of Fortune*, and the progress of the diary. As I am allowed only one visit a fortnight, this seems a sensible combination of business and pleasure, although I will miss not seeing James.

Phone Alison, who says she'll have finished typing *Volume One – Belmarsh: Hell* by Wednesday (70,000 words) and will post it to me immediately. She reminds me that from Monday she will be on holiday for two weeks. I need reminding. In prison you forget that normal people go on holiday.

When I return to my cell, I find David (whisky bootlegger) sweeping the corridor. I tell him about my water shortage. He offers me a large bottle of diet lemonade and a diet Robinsons blackcurrant juice in exchange for a £2 phonecard, which will give him a 43p profit. I accept, and we go off to his cell to complete the transaction. There is only one problem: you are not allowed to use phonecards for trading, because it might be thought you are a drug dealer. Each card has the prisoner's signature on the back of it, not unlike a credit card (see plate section).*

'No problem,' says David (he never swears). 'I can remove your name with Fairy Liquid and then replace it with mine.'

'How will you get hold of a bottle of Fairy Liquid?'

'I'm the wing cleaner.'

Silly question.

10.00 am

My pad-mate Jules has begun his education course today (life and social skills) so I have the cell to myself. I've been writing for only about thirty minutes when my door is unlocked and I'm told the prison probation officer wants to see me. I recall Tony's (absconding from Ford Open Prison) words when I was at Belmarsh: 'Don't act smart and find yourself on the wrong side of your probation officer, because they have considerable sway when it comes to deciding your parole date.'

I'm escorted to a private room, just a couple of doors away

---

* Some inmates sign their phonecards in pencil, as there is no prison rule against this. If there is a way around a regulation, a prisoner will find it.

from Mr Tinkler's office on the first-floor landing. I shake hands with a young lady who introduces herself as Lisa Dada. She is a blonde of about thirty and wearing a V-neck sweater that reveals she has just returned from holiday or spent a long weekend sitting in the sun. Like everyone else, she asks me how I am settling in. I tell her that I have no complaints other than the state of my cell, my rude introduction to rap music and window warriors.

Lisa begins by explaining that she has to see every prisoner, but there isn't much point in my case because her role doesn't kick in until six months before my parole.* 'And as I'm moving to Surrey in about two months' time,' she continues, 'to be nearer my husband who is a prison officer, you may well have moved to another establishment long before then, so I can't do much more than answer any questions you might have.'

'How did you meet your husband?' I ask.

'That's not the sort of question I meant,' she replies with a grin.

'He must be Nigerian.'

'What makes you think that?'

'Dada. It's an Igbo tribe name, the tribe of the leaders and warriors.'

She nods, and says, 'We met in prison in circumstances that sound as if they might have come from the pages of one of your novels.' I don't interrupt. 'I had a prisoner who was due to be released in the morning. The evening before, he was phoning his wife to arrange what time she should pick him up, but couldn't hear what she was saying because of the noise coming

---

*Parole: You are interviewed by a member of the Parole Board a few weeks before you have completed half your sentence, and their report can influence whether you should or should not be released.

from a TV in a nearby cell. He popped his head round the door and asked if the inmate could turn the volume down, and was told to "Fuck off". In a moment of anger he dropped the phone, walked into the cell and took a swing at the man. The inmate fell backwards onto the stone floor, cracked open his head and was dead before they could get him to a hospital. The first prison officer on the scene called for the assailant's probation officer, who happened to be me. We were married a year later.'

'What happened to the prisoner?' I ask.

'He was charged with manslaughter, pleaded guilty and was sentenced to three years. He served eighteen months. There was clearly no intent to murder. I know it sounds silly,' she adds, 'but until that moment, his record was unblemished.'

'So your husband is black. That can't have been easy for you, especially in prison.'

'No, it hasn't, but it helps me find a common thread with the dreadlocks.'*

'So what's it like being a thirty-something blonde probation officer?' I ask.

'It's not always easy,' she admits. 'Sixty per cent of the prisoners shout at me and tell me that I'm useless, while the other forty per cent burst into tears.'

'Burst into tears? That lot?' I say, thumbing towards the door.

'Oh, yes. I realize it's not a problem for you, but most of them spend their lives having to prove how macho they are, so when they come to see me it's the one chance they have to reveal their true feelings. Once they begin to talk about their families, their partners, children and friends, they often break down, suddenly aware that others might well be going through

----

* Dreadlocks is a term used by prisoners to describe a black man with long plaited hair.

an even more difficult time outside than they are locked up in here.'

'And the shouters, what do they imagine they're achieving?'

'Getting the rage out of their system. Such a disciplined regime creates pent-up emotions, and I'm often on the receiving end. I've experienced everything, including obscene language and explicit descriptions of what they'd like to do to me, while all the time staring at my breasts. One prisoner even unzipped his jeans and started masturbating. All that for twenty-one thousand a year.'

'So why do you do it?'

'I have the occasional success, perhaps one in ten, which makes it all seem worthwhile when you go home at night.'

'What's the worst part of your job?'

She pauses and thinks for a moment. 'Having to tell a prisoner that his wife or partner doesn't want him back just before they're due to be released.'

'I'm not sure I understand.'

'Many long-term prisoners phone their wives twice a week, and are even visited by them once a fortnight. But it's only when their sentence is drawing to a close and a probation officer has to visit the matrimonial home that the wife confesses she doesn't want her husband back. Usually because by then they are living with another man – sometimes their husband's best friend.'

'And they expect you to break the news?'

'Yes,' she replies. 'Because they can't face doing it themselves, even on the phone.'

'And is there any particular set of prisoners you don't like dealing with? The paedophiles, murderers, rapists, drug dealers, for example?'

'No, I can handle all of them,' she says. 'But the group I have no time for are the burglars.'

'Burglars?'

'They show neither remorse nor conscience. Even when they've stolen personal family heirlooms they tell you it's all right because the victim can claim it back on insurance.' She glances at her watch. 'I'm meant to be asking you some questions,' she pauses, 'not that the usual ones apply.'

'Try me,' I suggest. Lisa removes a sheet of paper from a file and reads out the listed questions.

'Are you married?, Are you living with your wife?, Have you any children?, Do you have any other children?, Are any of them in need of assistance or financial help?, Will you be returning to your family when you are released?, When you are released, do you have any income other than the ninety pounds the State provides for you?, Do you have somewhere to sleep on your first night out of prison?, Do you have a job to go to, with a guaranteed source of income?' She looks up. 'The purpose of the last question is to find out if you're likely to commit an offence within hours of leaving prison.'

'Why would anyone do that?' I ask.

'Because, for some of them, this is the only place that guarantees three meals a day, a bed and someone to talk to. You've got a good example on your wing. Out last month, back inside this month. Robbed an old lady of her bag and then immediately handed it back to her. He even hung around until the police arrived to make sure he was arrested.'

I think I know the prisoner she's referring to, and make a mental note to have a word with him. Our hour is drawing to a close, so I ask if she will stick with it.

'Yes. I've been in the service for ten years and, despite everything, it has its rewards. Mind you, it's changed a lot during the last decade. When I first joined, the motto emblazoned on our notepaper used to read, *Advise, Assist and Befriend*. Now it's

Enforcement, Rehabilitation and Public Protection; the result of a massive change in society, its new-found freedom and the citizen's demands for safety. The public doesn't begin to understand that at least thirty per cent of people in prison shouldn't be locked up at all, while seventy per cent, the professional criminals, will be in and out for the rest of their lives.'

There's a knock on the door. My hour's up, and we haven't even touched on the problem of drugs. Mr Chapman enters carrying two bundles of letters. Lisa looks surprised.

'That's only the first post,' Mr Chapman tells her.

'I can quite believe it,' she says. 'My parents send their best wishes. My father wanted you to sign one of his books, but I told him it would be most unprofessional.' I rise from my place. 'Good luck with your appeal,' she adds, as we shake hands. I thank her and return to my cell.

12 noon

Lunch: macaroni cheese and diet lemonade. I hate lemonade, so I spend some considerable time shaking the bottle in an effort to remove the bubbles. I have a considerable amount of time.

1.45 pm

Mr Chapman warns me that I will not be able to go to the gym this afternoon as I have to attend a CARAT (Counselling, Assessment, Referral, Advice and Through-care) meeting on drugs. This is another part of my induction. Despite the fact I've never touched a drug in my life, I can't afford to miss it. Otherwise I will never be moved from this filthy, dank, noisy wing. Naturally I comply.

2.00 pm

I try to pick up my books and notepads from reception only to be told by Mr Meanwell (a man who regularly reminds me 'Meanwell is my name, and mean well is my nature') that I can't have them because it's against prison regulations. All notepads and pens have to be purchased from the canteen and all books ordered through the library, who buy them direct from Waterstone's.

'But in Belmarsh they allowed me to have two notepads, two packets of pens and any number of books I required sent in, and they're a maximum-security prison.'

'I know,' says Meanwell with a smile. 'It's a damn silly rule, but there's nothing I can do about it.'

I thank him. Many of the senior officers know only too well what's sensible and what isn't, but are worried that if I receive what could be construed as special treatment it will be all over the tabloids the following morning. The rule is enforced because books, pads and pens are simply another way to smuggle in drugs. However, if I'm to go on writing, I'll have to purchase these items from the canteen, which means I'll need to cut down on Spam and Weetabix.

2.40 pm

I've been writing for about an hour when I am called to the CARAT meeting. Once again, eleven of us assemble in the room with the comfortable chairs. The CARAT representative is a young lady called Leah, who tells us that if we have any drug-related problems, she is there to advise and help. Leah reminds me of Mr Flintcroft, although she's pushing an even larger boulder up an even steeper hill.

I glance around the room at the other prisoners. Their faces are blank and resigned. I'm probably the only person present who has never taken a drug. The one comment Leah makes that catches the prisoners' attention is that if they were to have a period on D wing, the drug-free wing, it might even help with their parole. But before Leah can finish her sentence a ripple of laughter breaks out, and she admits that it's possible there are even more drugs on D wing than on A, B or C. Drug-free wings in most prisons have that reputation.*

When Leah comes to the end of her eight-minute discourse and invites questions, she is greeted with silence, the same silence Mr Flintcroft experienced.

I leave, feeling a little more cynical. Drugs are the biggest problem the Prison Service is currently facing, and not one prisoner has a question for the CARAT representative, let alone attempts to engage her in serious debate. However, I am relieved to observe that two inmates remain behind to have a private conversation with Leah.

6.00 pm

Kit change. Once a week you report to the laundry room for a change of sheets, pillowcases, towels and gym kit. I now have six towels and include four of them in my weekly change. They are all replaced, despite each prisoner only being allowed two. However, they won't replace my second pillowcase because you're allowed only one. I can't understand the logic of that.

You're meant to wash your own personal belongings, but I have already handed over that responsibility to Darren, who is

---

*This is yet another example of the implicit recognition by the Prison Service that over 70 per cent of inmates are on drugs.

the enhanced wing's laundry orderly. He picks up my bag of washing every Thursday, and returns it later that evening. He asks for no recompense. I must confess that the idea of washing my underpants in a sink shared with someone else's dirty cutlery isn't appealing.

6.30 pm

Supper. Unworthy of mention.

7.00 pm

Exercise. I walk round the perimeter of the yard with Darren and another inmate called Steve. Steve was convicted of conspiracy to murder. He is an accountant by profession, well spoken, intelligent and interesting company. His story turns out to be a fascinating one. He was a senior partner in a small successful firm of accountants. He fell in love with one of the other partners, who was already married to a colleague. One night, on his way home from work, Steve stopped at a pub he regularly frequented. He knew the barman well and told him that given half a chance he'd kill the bastard (meaning his girlfriend's husband). Steve thought nothing more of it until he received a phone call from the barman saying that for the right price it could be arranged. The phone call was being taped by the police, as were several others that followed. It was later revealed in court that the barman was already in trouble with the police and reported Steve in the hope that it would help have the charges against him dropped. It seems the key sentence that mattered was, 'Are you certain you want to go ahead with it?' which was repeated by the barman several times.

'Yes,' Steve always replied.

Steve and his girlfriend were arrested, pleaded guilty and were sentenced to seven years. She currently resides at High-point, while he has gone from A- to B- to C-cat status in a couple of years (record time), and is now living on the enhanced wing at Wayland with D-cat status. He doesn't want to move to an open prison because Wayland is near his home. He is also the prison's chief librarian. I have a feeling that you'll be hearing more about Steve in the future.

On the circuit round the perimeter we are joined by the prisoner I shared a cell with on my first night, Chris (stabbing with a Stanley knife). He tells me that the *News of the World* have been in touch with his mother and will be printing a story on Sunday. He tries to assure me that he has had no contact with them and his mother has said nothing.

'Then it will only be three pages,' I tell him.

When I return to my cell, Jules is looking worried. He's also heard that Chris will be featured in the *News of the World* this Sunday. Chris told him that a lot of his friends and associates don't even know he's in jail, and he doesn't want them to find out. He attends education classes twice a day and wants the chance to start a new life once he's been released. I just don't have the heart to tell him that the *News of the World* have absolutely no interest in his future.

10.00 pm

We watch the news. Still more August storms. At 10.30 Jules switches channels to *Ally McBeal* while I try unsuccessfully to sleep. I'm not sure which is more distracting, the TV in our cell, or the rap music emanating from the other side of the block.

DAY 29   THURSDAY 16 AUGUST 2001

5.50 am

I wake from a dream in which I had been using the most foul language when talking to Mary. I can't explain it. I write for a couple of hours.

8.00 am

I plug in Jules's radio so that I can hear Mary's interview with John Humphrys. I shave while the news is on, and become more and more nervous. It's always the same. I am very anxious when William screens one of the documentaries he's been working on, or James is running the 800 metres, and especially whenever Mary has to give a talk that lay people might expect to understand. She's first on after the news and handles all of John Humphrys' questions in that quiet academic way that could only impress an intelligent listener. But I can tell, even after her first reply, just how nervous she is. Once Mary has dealt with the Kurds and Baroness Nicholson, Humphrys moves on to the subject of how I'm getting on in jail. That was when Mary should have said, 'My agreement with you, Mr Humphrys, was to discuss only matters arising from the Kurds.' Once Mary failed to point this out, he moved on to the trial, the appeal and the sentence. I had warned her that he would. He has no interest in keeping to any agreement made between her and the producer. And that's why he is such a sharp interviewer, as I know from past experience.

9.30 am

I call Mary, who feels she was dreadful and complains that John Humphrys broke the BBC's agreement and once the piece was over she told him so. What does he care? She then tells me that the CEO of the Red Cross, Sir Nicholas Young, was interviewed later, and was uncompromising when it came to any suggestion that one penny raised for the Kurds in the UK had not been accounted for. He went on to point out that I had nothing to do with either the collecting or distribution of any monies. I suggest to Mary that perhaps the time has come to sue Baroness Nicholson. Mary tells me that the lawyer's first priority is to have my D-cat reinstated so I can be moved to an open prison before we issue the writ. Good thinking.

'Don't waste any more of your units,' she says. 'See you tomorrow.'

9.50 am

Disaster. Darren reappears with my washing. All fresh and clean, but the dryer has broken down for the first time in living memory. I take the wet clothes back to my cell and hang the T-shirts on the end of the bed, my underwear from an open cupboard door and my socks over the single chair. The sun is shining, but not many of its rays are reaching through the bars and into my cell.

10.00 am

Today is the first day of the fourth test match against Australia, and Hussain is back as captain. He said that although we've lost the Ashes (3–0), English pride is now at stake. I write for an hour and then turn on the television at eleven to see who won the toss. It's been raining all morning. Of course it has; the match is at Headingley (Leeds). I switch off the television and return to my script.

11.40 am

I've been writing for over an hour when the cell door is unlocked. The governor would like a word. I go to the interview room and find Mr Carlton-Boyce and Mr Tinkler waiting for me.

Mr Carlton-Boyce looks embarrassed when he tries to explain why I can't have any writing pads and pens or Alan Clark's *Diaries*. I make a small protest but only so it's on the record. He then goes on to tell me that I will not be moving to C block after all. They've had a re-think, and I'll be joining the adults on the enhanced spur, but – and there is always a but in prison – as no one is being released until 29 August, I'll have to stay put until then.

I thank him, and ask if my room-mate Jules can be moved to a single cell, as I fear it can't be too long before the *News of the World* will do to him exactly what they've done to every other prisoner who has shared a cell with me. This shy, thoughtful man will end up being described as a drug baron, and he doesn't have any way of fighting back.

Governor Carlton-Boyce nods. Promises are never made in prison, but he does go as far as saying, 'The next thing on my agenda is cell dispersal, because we have eight more prisoners coming in tomorrow.' I thank him and leave, aware that's about the biggest hint I'll get.

12 noon

Lunch. Dale passes me two little sealed boxes, rather than the usual single portion, and winks. I was down on today's menu for number three – vegetable stew – but when I get back to my cell, I discover the other box contains mushroom soup. So I linger over the soup followed by vegetable stew. It's not Le Caprice – but it's not Belmarsh either.

1.15 pm

I'm told that as part of my induction I must report to the education department and take a reading, writing and numeracy test. When I take my seat in the classroom and study the forms, it turns out to be exactly the same test as the one set at Belmarsh. Should I tell them that I took the papers only two weeks ago, or should I just get on with it? I can see the headline in the *Mirror*: Archer Refuses to Take Writing Test. It would be funny if it wasn't exactly what the *Mirror* would do.* I get on with it.

3.15 pm

Gym. It's circuit-training day, and I manage about half of the set programme – known as the dirty dozen. The youngsters are good, but the star turns out to be a forty-five-year-old gypsy,†

---

* If you want to study the details of the test, they're described in *Volume One – Belmarsh: Hell*.
† I later learn from an officer that it's politically incorrect to describe anyone as a gypsy nowadays. They prefer to be called travellers.

who is covered in tattoos, and serving an eleven-year sentence for drug dealing. He's called Minnie, and out-runs them, out-jumps them, out-lifts them, out-presses them, and isn't even breathing heavily at the end. He puts me to shame; I can only hope that the youngsters feel equally humiliated.

4.20 pm

I'm back in time for a shower. David (whisky bootlegger) is standing by my door. He tells me that he's written the outline for a novel and wants to know how to get in contact with a ghostwriter. This is usually a surrogate for are you available? I tell him exactly what I tell anyone else who writes to me on this subject (three or four letters a week): go to your local library, take out a copy of *The Writers' and Artists' Yearbook* and you'll find a section listing agents who handle ghostwriters. I assume that will keep him quiet for a few days.

4.41 pm

David returns clutching a copy of *The Writers' and Artists' Yearbook* and shows me a page of names. I glance down the list but none is familiar. I have come across only a handful of agents over the years – Debbie Owen, George Greenfield, Deborah Rodgers, Jonathan Lloyd and Ed Victor – but there must be at least another thousand I've never heard of. I suggest that as my agent is visiting me tomorrow, if he selects some names, I'll ask Jonathan if he knows any of them.

4.56 pm

David returns with the list of names written out on a single sheet of paper. He hands over a Diet Coke. He's what Simon Heffer would describe as 'a proper gent'.

6.00 pm

Supper. Vegetable pie, two boiled potatoes and a lump of petits pois, making *un seul pois*.

I switch on the TV. Australia are 241 for 3, and Ponting is 144 not out. Together with Waugh, they've put on 170. I switch off. Why did I ever switch on?

After supper, I go down to the Association room to find Dale (wounding with intent) and Jimmy (transporting Ecstasy tablets) playing snooker for a Mars bar.* It's the first time I've seen Jimmy beaten at anything, and what's more, he's being thrashed by a far superior player. It's a subject I know a little about as I was President of the World Snooker Association before I was convicted. Jimmy whispers in my ear, 'Dale beats everyone, but like any hungry animal, he has to be fed at least twice a day. We take it in turns to hand over a Mars bar. It's a cheap way of keeping him under control.' In case you've forgotten, Dale is six foot three and weighs twenty-seven stone.

After the game is over, the three of us join Darren in the exercise yard. Dale manages only one circuit before heading back in, exhausted, while the three of us carry on for the full forty-five minutes. During the second circuit, I tell them about Derek, who did the drawing of my cell (*Belmarsh*), and ask if

---

* The accepted tariff for almost all bets in prison is a Mars bar (30p).

they know of any artists in Wayland. Jimmy tells me that there is a brilliant (his word) artist on C block. I ask if he will introduce me.

'Be warned, he's weird,' says Jimmy, 'and can be very rude if he takes against you.'

I tell Jimmy that I've been dealing with artists for the past thirty-five years and I've never met one who could be described as normal. It's all part of their appeal.

'I feel like a drink,' says Darren as the evening sun continues to beat down on us. 'Know anyone who's got some hooch?' he asks Jimmy.

'Hooch?' I say. 'What's that?'

They both laugh, a laugh that suggests I still have much to learn. 'Every block,' says Darren, 'has a hotplate man, a cleaner, a tea-boy and a painter. They're all appointed by the screws and are paid around twelve pounds a week. Every block also has a drug dealer, a haircutter, a clothes-washer and a brewer. C block has the best brewer – for a two-pound phonecard, you can get half a litre of hooch.'

'But what's it made of?'

'The ingredients are normally yeast, sugar, water and orange juice. It's harder to produce during the summer months because you need the hot pipes that run through your cell to be boiling in order to ferment the brew, so it's almost impossible to get decent hooch in August.'

'What's it taste like?'

'Awful, but at least it's guaranteed to get you drunk,' says Jimmy. 'Which kills off a few more hours of your sentence, even if you wake up with one hell of a hangover.'

'If you're desperate,' Darren adds, 'fresh orange juice is still on the canteen list.'

'How does that help?'

'Just leave it on your window ledge in the sun for a few days, and you'll soon find out.'

'But where can you hide the hooch once you've made it?'

'We used to have the perfect hiding place,' Darren pauses, 'but unfortunately they discovered it.'

Jimmy smiles as I wait for an explanation. 'One Sunday morning,' Darren continues, 'the number one brewer on our spur was found roaming around inebriated. When breathalysed, he registered way above the limit. The drug squad were called in, and every cell on the spur was stripped bare, but no alcohol of any kind was discovered. His hiding place would have remained a mystery if a small fire hadn't broken out in the kitchen. An officer grabbed the nearest fire extinguisher and pointed it in the direction of the blaze, only to find that the flames leapt even higher. An immediate halt was called by the chef who fortunately understood the effects of ethanol, otherwise the prison might have been razed to the ground. A full enquiry was held, and three inmates were shipped out to different B-cats the following morning, "on suspicion of producing hooch".'

'In fact,' said Darren, 'It wasn't hooch they were guilty of brewing. This particular strain of neat alcohol had been made by filtering metal polish through six slices of bread into a plastic mug in the hope of removing any impurities.'

I feel sick, without even having to sample the brew.

Jimmy goes on to point out that not only are some inmates brighter than the officers, but they also have twenty-four hours every day to think up such schemes, while the screws have to get on with their job.

'But the best hooch I ever tasted,' said Darren, 'had a secret ingredient.'

'And what was that, may I ask?'

'Marmite. But once the screws caught on to how much yeast it contained, they took it off the canteen list.' He pauses. 'So now we just steal the yeast from the kitchen.'

'Damn,' I said. 'I like Marmite; it was on the Belmarsh canteen list.'

'I don't think that's a good enough reason, my lord, to be transferred back to Belmarsh,' says Darren. 'Mind you,' he adds, 'perhaps I should have a word with the governor, now it's known that you are partial to it.'

I kick him gently up the backside as an officer is passing in the opposite direction.

'Did you see that, Mr Chapman? Archer is bullying me.'

'I'll put him on report, and he'll be back in Belmarsh by the end of the week,' Mr Chapman promises.

We laugh as we continue on the perimeter circuit. However, I point out how easy it is to make an accusation, and how long it takes to refute it. It's been a month since Emma Nicholson appeared on *Newsnight* insinuating that I had stolen money intended for the Kurds, and it will probably be another month before the police confirm there is no case to answer.

'But just think about that for a minute, Jeffrey. If it hadn't been for that bitch Nicholson, you would never have met Jimmy and me, who have not only added greatly to your knowledge of prison life, but enabled a further volume to be written.'

7.30 pm

One of the officers says there's a package for me in the office. I'm puzzled as I've already had my mail for today, and registered letters are always opened in front of two officers, around eleven each morning. When I walk in, he makes a point of closing the office door before he hands over a copy of Alan Clark's *Diaries*, a pad and a book of stamps. Someone else who considers the regulations damned stupid.

He goes on to say that my wife will be searched when she visits the prison tomorrow. 'We're all embarrassed about it,' he adds, 'but it will be no worse than at an airport. But perhaps it might be wise to let her know. By the way, the press are still hanging about hoping to catch her when she arrives.' I thank him and leave.

8.00 pm

I read a few pages of the Clark *Diaries*, which I enjoy every bit as much a second time. I also enjoyed Alan's company, and will never forget a dinner party he gave at Saltwood just before the general election in 1997. Alan posed the question to his guests, 'What do you think the majority will be at the next election?' Most of the assembled gathering thought Labour would win by over a hundred.* The only dissenter was Michael Howard, who was Home Secretary at the time. He put up a bold defence of John Major's administration, and told his fellow guests that he felt it was still possible for the Conservatives to win the next election. Alan told him that if he really believed that, he was living in cloud cuckoo land. I don't know to this day if Michael was simply being loyal to the prime minister. Although I can tell you that, like John Major, he is one of those people who doesn't cross over to the other side of the road when you're in trouble.

---

* Selina Scott said that Labour would win by over 150, and she was closest to the final result.

10.00 pm

Suddenly feel very hungry – eat a bowl of cornflakes and a Mars bar. Check my clothes – still not dry. I don't bother with another of John Mortimer's great trials. Feel I have enough murderers surrounding me without having to read about them.

DAY 30   FRIDAY 17 AUGUST 2001

6.09 am

The first thing I notice when I wake is that my Mach3 razor has disappeared. The wash basin is next to the door. In future, after I've shaved, I'll have to hide it in my cupboard. It would have to be stolen on the day Mary is visiting me; I want to be clean shaven but I don't want to cut myself to ribbons with a prison razor. It also reminds me that, because I hadn't expected to be convicted, I've been wearing my Longines watch for the past month, and I must hand it over to my son during the visit this afternoon.

8.15 am

Breakfast. Before I go down to the hotplate, I extract a letter from yesterday's mail that is in Spanish. Dale has told me that one of the servers on the hotplate hails from Colombia, so he should be able to translate it for me. His name is Sergio, and he usually stands quietly on the end of the line, handing out the fruit. I pass the missive across to him, and ask if we could meet later. He nods, and hands me a banana in return.

9.00 am

Today's induction is education, once again held in the room with the comfy chairs. For the first time the other prisoners show some interest. Why? Because this is how they'll earn their weekly wage. The head of education introduces herself as Wendy. She must be in her fifties, has curly grey hair, wears a flowery blouse, white skirt and sensible shoes. She has the air of a headmistress.

Wendy wheels a little projector up to the front, and begins a slide show. Using the white brick wall as a backdrop, she shows us what her department has to offer. The first slide reveals five options:

Basic skills
English as an additional language
Social and life skills
Business skills
Art, craft and design

'Education,' Wendy points out, 'is part-time (one session a day), so you can only earn seven pounds thirty-five per week.' The other prisoners don't take a great deal of interest in this slide, but immediately perk up when the second chart flashes on to the wall. VT and CIT training courses:

Bricklaying
Plumbing
Electrical installation
Painting and decorating
Welding
Motor mechanics
Light vehicle body repair
Industrial cleaning
Computer application

The weekly pay for any one of these courses is also £7.35, but does give you a basic training for when you return to the outside world.

When the final slide comes up, most of the inmates begin licking their collective lips, because this offers not only real earning power, but a position of responsibility plus perks. The extra money guarantees a more substantial canteen list each week (extra tobacco) and even the opportunity to save something for when you are released. The slide reveals:

Plastic recycling £10.15 per week
Ration packing £9.35
Gardening (one of the most sought-after jobs, with a long waiting list) £9.00
General cleaner £6.70
Works £8.50
Kitchen £8.50
Stores (very popular, longer waiting list than the MCC) £10.00
Chapel £8.00
Drug rehabilitation unit £6.70

Before she can turn back to face her audience, the questions come thick and fast. Wendy points out that most of these jobs already have waiting lists, even washing-up, as there are far more prisoners than jobs. Wendy handles the questions sympathetically, without giving anyone false hopes of being offered one of these more remunerative positions.

Her final task is to hand round more forms to be filled in. My fellow inmates grab them, and then take some time considering their options. I put a cross next to 'pottery' in the education box, but add that I would be happy to do a creative writing course, or teach other prisoners to read and write. Wendy has already pointed out that the education department is understaffed. However, she tells me that such an initiative would require the governor's approval, and she'll get back to me. I return to my cell.

11.00 am

I report to the gym to assist with the special needs group. They are about thirty in number, and I've been put in charge of four of them: Alex, Robbie, Les and Paul. Three head straight for the rowing machines, while Alex places himself firmly on the treadmill. He sets off at one mile an hour and, with coaxing and patience (something I don't have in abundance), he manages two miles an hour. I have rarely seen such delight on a competitor's face. This, for Alex, is his Olympic gold medal. I then suggest he moves on to the step machine while I try to tempt Paul off the rower and onto the running machine. I have to give him several demonstrations as to how it works before he'll even venture on, and when he finally does, we start him off at half a mile an hour. By using sign language – hands waving up and down – we increase his speed to one mile an hour. I next try to show him how to use the plus and minus buttons. He conquers this new skill by the time he's walked half a mile. While I teach him how to operate the machine, he teaches me to be patient. By the time he's done a mile, Paul has mastered the technique completely, and feels like a king. I feel pretty good too.

I look around the room and observe the other prisoners – murderers, drug barons, armed robbers and burglars, gaining just as much from the experience as their charges.

Our final session brings all the group together in the gym where we play a game that's a cross between cricket and football, called catchball. A plastic ball is bowled slowly along the ground to a child (I must remember that though they think like children, they are not), who kicks it in the air, and then takes a run. If they are caught, they're out, and someone else takes their place. One of the players, Robbie, catches almost everything, whether it flies above his head, at his feet, or straight at him. This is always greeted with yelps of delight.

By eleven thirty, we're all exhausted. The group are then ushered out of a special door at the side of the gym. The boys shake hands and the girls cuddle their favourite prisoner. Carl, a handsome West Indian, gets more cuddles than any of us (they see no colour, only kindness). As they leave to go home, they enquire how long you will be there, and thus I discover why prisoners with longer sentences are selected for this particular responsibility.* I make a bold attempt to escape with the group, who all laugh and point at me. When we reach the waiting bus, Mr Maiden finally calls me back.

12 noon

Lunch. I can't remember what I've just eaten because I'm glued to the morning papers. Mary is given rave reviews right across the board – dozens of column inches praising the way she handled John Humphrys.

Lord Longford's reported dying words, 'Free Jeffrey Archer', get a mention in almost every column. I didn't know Frank Longford well, but enjoyed his wife's reply to Roy Plomley on *Desert Island Discs*:

Plomley: 'Lady Longford, have you ever considered divorce?'

---

* Sex offenders who elect *not* to be placed on E wing but with the main prison population are never permitted to work with the special needs group.

Lady Longford: 'No, never. Murder several times, but divorce, never.'

I have a feeling Mary would have given roughly the same reply.

2.00 pm

I am watching the Australians leave the field – they were all out for 447 – when the cell door is unlocked and I'm told to report to the visitors' area. I switch off the TV and head out into the corridor. How unlike Belmarsh. I even have to ask the way. 'Take the same route as you would for the gym,' says Mr Chapman, 'but then turn right at the end of the corridor.'

When I arrive, the two duty officers don't strip search me, and show no interest in my watch, which is secreted under my shirtsleeve. For visits, all prisoners have to wear striped blue prison shirts and blue jeans.

The visitors' room is about the same size as the gym and is filled with seventy small round tables, each surrounded by four chairs – one red, three blue. The red chair and the table are bolted together so there is always a gap between you and your visitor. This is to prevent easy passing of illicit contraband. The prisoner sits in the red seat, with his back to the officers. In the middle of each table is a number. I'm fourteen. There is a tuck shop on the far side of the room where visitors can purchase non-alcoholic drinks, chocolate and crisps. The one prisoner trusted to handle cash in the shop is Steve (conspiracy to murder, librarian and accountant) – would-be murderer he may be, thief he is not. Once every prisoner has been seated, the visitors are allowed in.

I watch the different prisoners' wives, partners, girlfriends and children as they walk through the door and try to guess which table they'll go to. Wrong almost every time. Mary's about fifth through the gate. She is wearing a long white dress which shows off that glorious mop of dark hair. Will is only a pace behind, followed by my agent and close friend, Jonathan Lloyd. He and Will take a seat near the door, so that Mary and I can have a little time to ourselves.

Mary brings me up to date with what's happening at the Red Cross. Their CEO, Sir Nicholas Young, has been most supportive; no fence-sitter he. Because of his firm statements Mary feels confident that it won't be long before I am moved on to an open prison. She also feels that the Prison Service and the police have been put in an embarrassing position, and will fall back on claiming that they had no choice but to follow up Nicholson's accusation. The Red Cross may even consider taking legal action against her. The lawyers' advice is, if they do, we should remain on the sidelines. I agree. She beckons to Will who comes over to join us.

Will tells me that he's been monitoring everything, and although it's tough for me, they are both working daily on my behalf. I confess that there are times in the dead of night when you wonder if anyone is out there. But I realize when it comes to back-up, there can't be a prisoner alive with a more supportive family. When Will's completed his report, Jonathan is finally allowed to join us, while Will goes off to purchase six Diet Cokes and a bottle of Highland Spring. (Three of the Cokes are for me.)

Jonathan has travelled up to Wayland to discuss my latest novel. He also wants an update on the diaries. I'm able to tell him that Belmarsh is completed (70,000 words) although I still need to read it through once again, but hope to have it on his desk in about two weeks' time.

We discuss selling the newspaper rights separately, while allowing my publisher a 10 per cent topping right* on the three volumes, as they've been so good to me in the past. But we all agree that nothing should happen until we know the outcome of my appeal, both for conviction and sentence.

Once Jonathan feels his business is complete, he retires once again, so that I can spend the last half hour with Mary and Will. When we're alone, we recap on all that needs to be done before we meet again in a fortnight's time. At least I now have enough phonecards to keep in regular touch.

Steve comes across to clear our table – it's the first time Mary has met someone convicted of conspiracy to murder. This tall, elegant man 'looks more like a company secretary than a would-be murderer' is her only comment. 'You probably pass a murderer on the street once a week,' I suggest.

'Time for visitors to leave,' announces a voice behind me. I unstrap my Longines watch to exchange it for a twenty-dollar Swatch I purchased in a rash moment at Washington airport. Will is facing the two officers, who are seated on a little platform behind me. He nods, and we both put on our new watches.

'All visitors must now leave,' repeats the officer politely but firmly. We begin our long goodbyes and Mary is among the last to depart.

When I leave the room, the officer asks me to take off my shoes, which he checks carefully, but doesn't ask me to remove anything else, including my socks. He shows no interest in my watch and nods me through.

---

* After the final bid has come in, my publisher would be allowed to offer 10 per cent more and automatically be granted the rights.

DAY 30

4.17 pm

Back in my cell, I find my canteen order has been left on the end of the bed. Hip, hip, and my clothes are finally dry, hooray. As I unpack my wares, Dale arrives with back-up provisions.

6.00 pm

Supper. Beans and chips accompanied by a large mug of Volvic.

7.00 pm

Exercise. Dale joins Jimmy, Darren and me as we walk around the yard, and manages all three circuits. On the last one, he spots the artist he told me about yesterday. He is sitting in the far corner sketching a prisoner. An inmate is leaning up against the fence in what he assumes is a model's pose. We walk across to take a look. The drawing is excellent, but the artist immediately declares that he's not happy with the result. I've never known an artist say anything else. As he's more than fully occupied, we agree to meet tomorrow evening at the same time.

When I return to the wing, Sergio (hotplate, Colombian) asks me if I would like to join him in his cell on the enhanced spur. He's kindly translated the letter from the Spanish student; it seems that the young man has just finished a bachelor's degree and needs a loan if he's to consider going on to do a doctorate. I thank Sergio, and pen a note on the bottom of the letter, so that Alison can reply.

'Lock up,' bellows an officer. Just as I'm about to depart, Sergio asks, 'Can we talk again sometime, as there's something else I'd like to discuss with you?' I nod, wondering what this quiet Colombian can possibly want to see me about.

DAY 31 SATURDAY 18 AUGUST 2001

6.21 am

Had a bad night. There was an intake of young prisoners yesterday afternoon, and several of them turned out to be window warriors. They spent most of the night letting everyone know what they would like to do to Ms Webb, the young woman officer on night duty. Ms Webb is a charming, university-educated woman who is on the fast-track for promotion. Darren told me that whenever a new group of prisoners comes in, they spend the first twenty-four hours sorting out the 'pecking order'. At night, Wayland is just as uncivilized as Belmarsh, and the officers show no interest in doing anything about it. After all, the governor is sound asleep in her bed.

At Belmarsh I was moved into a single cell after four days. In Wayland I've been left for eleven days among men whose every second word is 'fuck', some of whom have been charged with murder, rape, grievous bodily harm and drug pushing. Let me make it clear: this is not the fault of the prison officers on the ground, but the senior management. There are prisoners who have been incarcerated in Wayland for some time and have never once seen the governor. I do not think that all the officers have met her. That's not what I call leadership.

DAY 31

One of yesterday's new intake thought it would be clever to slam my door closed just after an officer had unlocked it so that I could go to breakfast. He then ran up and down the corridor shouting, 'I locked Jeffrey Archer in, I locked Jeffrey Archer in.' Luckily, only a few of the prisoners are this moronic, but they still make everyone else's life unbearable.

8.15 am

Breakfast. One look at the lumpy, powdered scrambled egg and a tomato swimming in water and I'm off. As I leave, Sergio suggests we meet in his room at 10.30. I nod my agreement.

9.00 am

Saturday is a dreadful day in prison. It's the weekend and you think about what you and your family might have been doing together. However, because we are 'unlocked' during the day, but 'banged up' in the early evening, there is always a queue outside my cell door: prisoners wanting letters written, queries answered, or on the scrounge for phonecards and stamps. At least no one bothers to ask me for tobacco. So on a Saturday, my only chance of a clear two hours to write are between six and eight in the morning, and six and eight at night.

10.00 am

I call Chris Beetles at his gallery. It's the opening of his Cat Show, – these ones are in frames not cages – so I don't waste a lot of his time, and promise I'll call him back on Monday.

On my way back to the cell I pass Darren in the corridor and stop to ask him about Sergio, whose cell is three doors away from his.

'A real gentleman,' says Darren. 'Keeps himself to himself. In fact I don't know much more about him now than I did when he arrived at Wayland a year ago. He's a Colombian, but he's one of the few prisoners who never touches drugs. He doesn't even smoke. You'll like him.'

10.30 am

When I arrive at Sergio's cell he checks his watch as if he assumed I'd be on time. If the Archer theory is correct – namely that you can tell everything you need to know about a prisoner from his cell – then Sergio is a neat and tidy man who likes everything in its place. He offers me his chair, while he sits on the bed. His English is good, although not fluent, and it quickly becomes clear that he has no idea who I am, which helps considerably.

When I tell him I'm a writer, he looks interested. I promise to have one of my books (Spanish translation) sent in. An hour passes before he tells me anything about himself. He makes it clear, as if he wants the world to know, that Colombians fall into two categories: those who are involved in drugs and those who are not. He and his family come into the latter group, and he seems genuinely pleased when I tell him that I have an aversion to drugs that is bordering on the manic.

His family, he tells me, have no idea he's in jail.* In fact his weekly call to Bogotá accounts for almost his entire income. He's divorced with no children, so the only people he has to fool are his brother, his sister and his parents. They believe he has a responsible job with an import/export company in London. He

---

* Sergio is not his real name.

will return to Bogotá in five weeks' time. There is no need for him to purchase a plane ticket, as he will be deported. Were he ever to return to Britain, he would immediately be arrested, put back in jail, and would remain locked up until he had completed the other half of his eight-year sentence. He has no plans to come back, he tells me.

The conversation drifts from subject to subject, to see if we can find anything of mutual interest. He has a great knowledge of emeralds, coffee and bananas – three subjects of which I know virtually nothing, other than their colour. It's then I spot a photograph of him with, he tells me, his mother and sister. A huge smile comes over my face as he removes the picture from the shelf to allow me a closer look.

'Is that a Botero?' I ask, squinting at the painting behind his mother. He cannot hide his surprise that I should ever have heard of the maestro.

'Yes it is,' he says. 'My mother is a friend of Botero.'

I almost leap in the air, as I have long dreamed of adding a Botero to my art collection in London or my sculpture collection in Grantchester. In fact Chris Beetles and I travelled to Calabria two years ago to visit the great man at his foundry. Sergio quickly reveals that he knows a considerable amount about Latin American art, and names several other artists including Manzù, Rivera and Betancourt. He has met Botero, and his family are friends of Manzù. I tell him I would love to own one of their works, but both artists are way out of my price range, particularly Botero, who is considered to be the Picasso of South America. The French think so highly of him that they once held an exhibition of his sculptures along the Champs-Elysées; the first time a foreigner has been so honoured.

'It's just possible I could find one of his works at a price you could afford.'

'How is that possible?' I ask.

Sergio then explains to me at great length what he calls the 'Colombian mentality'.

'To start with, you have to accept that my countrymen only want to deal in cash. They do not trust banks, and do not believe in cheques, which is why they regularly alternate between being rich and penniless. When they are wealthy, they buy everything in sight – jewellery, yachts, cars, houses, paintings, women, anything; when they are poor they sell everything, and the women leave them. But Colombians have no fear of selling,' he continues, 'because they always believe that they will be rich again ... tomorrow, when they will buy back everything, even the women. I know a trader in Bogotá,' he continues, 'who bought a Botero for a million dollars, and five years later sold it for two hundred thousand cash. Give me time and I'll come up with a Botero at the right price,' he pauses, 'but I would expect something in return.'

Am I about to find out if Sergio is a con artist, or as Darren suggested, 'a real gentleman'?

'I have a problem,' he adds. 'I have been in jail for four years, and when I finish half my sentence I will be deported.' I'm trying to write notes as he speaks. 'I will be put on a plane without any presents for my three nephews and niece.' I don't interrupt. 'Would it be possible for you to get me three Manchester United shirts for the nephews – seven, ten and eleven years old – and a *Lion King* outfit for my eight-year-old niece?'

'Anything else?' I ask.

'Yes, I need a suitcase, because all I have is a HMP Wayland plastic bag, and,' he hesitates, 'I also need twenty pounds in phonecards so I can call Bogotá and not worry about being cut off.'

'Is that it?'

He hesitates once more. 'I would like one hundred pounds put in my prison account so I can pick up one or two things for my family at the airport. I don't want them to wonder why I don't have any presents for them.'

I consider his requests. For risk capital investment of around £200 I would have an outside chance of owning a Botero I can afford. I nod to show that I agree to his terms.

'If you do this for me,' he adds, 'I will tell you more. In fact I have already told you more in an hour than I have any other prisoner in four years.' He then writes down the name and address of a contact in London and says, 'Give her the suitcase, the T-shirts and the one hundred pounds, and she will send them on to me at Wayland. That way you won't be involved.'

11.44 am

I phone a friend who used to work in the T-shirt business, and pass on the order for Manchester United T-shirts and a *Lion King* outfit. He sounds intrigued, but doesn't ask any questions. I then call my driver at home and explain that the items are to be delivered to a flat in north London, along with £100 in cash. 'Consider it done,' he says.

11.51 am

I cross the corridor to Dale's room and tell him I need twenty pounds' worth of phonecards.

'Just like that, my lord?'

'Just like that,' I reply. 'Put it on my account and I'll have the money sent through to you.'

He opens a drawer and removes ten £2 cards and passes them across. 'You've wiped me out,' he says.

'Then get back to work, because I have a feeling I'm going to need even more next week.'

'Why? Are you calling America?'

'Right idea. Wrong continent.'

I leave Dale and return to Sergio's room. I hand over the ten phonecards and tell him that the other items will all have been delivered by this time tomorrow. He looks astonished.

'How fortunate that you are sent to this jail, just as I am leaving.'

I confess that I hadn't seen it quite that way, and remind him that we have a deal.

'One Botero, at a price you can afford, within a year,' he confirms. 'You'll have it by Christmas.'

When I leave him to return to my cell, I remember just how much I miss dealing, whether it's for £200 or £2 million. I once watched Jimmy Goldsmith bargaining for a backgammon board with a street trader in Mexico. It took him all of forty minutes, and he must have saved every penny of £10, but he just couldn't resist it.

12 noon

Lunch. I devour a plate of Princes ham (49p) surrounded by prison beans while I watch England avoid the follow on.*

2.00 pm

I head for the library – closed, followed by the gym – cancelled. So I'll have to settle for a forty-five-minute walk around the exercise yard.

---

* If you don't understand 'follow on', it would take a chapter to explain. Just be assured, it's not good.

3.00 pm

The man who was sketching the portrait of another prisoner yesterday is waiting for me as Darren, Jimmy and I walk out into the yard. He introduces himself as Shaun, but tells me that most inmates call him Sketch. I explain that I want a portrait of Dale (wounding with intent), Darren (marijuana only), Jimmy (Ecstasy courier), Steve (conspiracy to murder) and Jules (drug dealing) for the diary; a sort of montage. He looks excited by the commission, but warns me that he'll have to get on with it as he's due to be released in three weeks' time.

'Any hope of some colour?' I ask.

'Follow me,' he says. We troop across rough grass littered with rubbish and uneaten food to end up outside a cell window on the ground floor of C wing. I stare through the bars at paintings that cover almost all his wall space. There's even a couple on the bed. I'm left in no doubt that he's the right man for the job.

'How about a picture of the prison?' he suggests.

'Yes,' I tell him, 'especially if it's from your window, because I have an almost identical view two blocks over.' (See plate section.)

I then ask him how he would like to be paid. Shaun suggests that as he is leaving soon, it may be easier to send a cheque directly to his home, so his girlfriend can bank it. He says he'd like to think about a price overnight and discuss it with me during exercise tomorrow; I'm not allowed to visit his cell as he resides on another block so we can only talk through his barred window.*

---

* In theory, this is to prevent the movement of drugs from block to block, but I don't know why they bother, because every prisoner knows exactly which window to go to if they want a fix. Just as I go up to C wing, third window on the left, to view Shaun's pictures, some of the prisoners are, at this moment, queuing outside the next window to purchase their drugs.

5.00 pm

Supper: vegetable stir-fry and a mug of Volvic.

I've negotiated two art deals today, so I feel a little better. Because the library was closed and I have finished *The Glass Bead Game*, I have nothing new to read until it opens again tomorrow. I spend the rest of the evening writing about Sergio.

DAY 32   SUNDAY 19 AUGUST 2001

5.59 am

First peaceful night in weeks. Yesterday I visited the three prisoners with noisy stereos and the two inmates who go on shouting at each other all through the night. But not before I had been asked to do so by several other prisoners on the spur. I got two surprises: firstly, no one was willing to accompany me – they were all happy to point out which cells they were in, but no more than that. The second surprise was that all of the transgressors, without exception, responded favourably to my courteous request with either, 'Not me, gov,' or, 'Sorry, Jeff, I'll turn it down,' and in one case, 'I'll turn it off at nine, Jeff.' Interesting.

8.15 am

Breakfast. A prisoner in the queue for the hotplate asks me if I'm moving cells today.

'No,' I tell him. 'What makes you think that?'

'The name card outside your cell has disappeared, always the first sign that you're on the move.'

I laugh, and explain, 'It's been removed every day – a sort of talisman of my existence. I seem to be the only thing that doesn't move.'

When I reach the hotplate Dale gives a curt nod, a sign he needs to see me; Sergio also nods. I leave the hotplate empty-handed, bar a slice of toast and two appointments. I return to my cell and eat a bowl of my cornflakes with my milk.

9.15 am

Gym. The treadmill is not working again, so I start with the rower and manage 1,956 metres in ten minutes. I would have done better if I hadn't started chatting to the inmate on the next rower. All across his back is tattooed the word MONSTER, though, in truth, he's softly spoken and, whenever I've come across him in the corridor, friendly. I ask what his real name is.

'Martin,' he whispers, 'but only my mother calls me that. Everyone else calls me Monster.' He's managed 2,470 metres in ten minutes despite chatting to me.

He tells me that in January, when he arrived at Wayland, he weighed seventeen and a half stone. He is a taxi driver from Essex, and admits that it was easy to put on weight in that job. Now he tips the scales at thirteen stone five pounds, and his girlfriend has to visit him every two weeks just to make sure that she'll still recognize him when he's released. He was sentenced to three years for transporting cannabis from one Ilford club to another.

About a third of the men in this prison have been convicted of some crime connected with cannabis, and most of them will say, I repeat *say*, that they would never deal in hard drugs. In fact, Darren goes further and, snarling, adds that he would try to dissuade anyone who did. If cannabis were to be legalized – and for most of the well-rehearsed reasons, I remain unconvinced that it should – the price would fall by around 70 per cent, tax revenues would be enormous and prison numbers would drop overnight.

Many young prisoners complain, 'It's your lot who are smoking the stuff, Jeff. In ten years' time it won't even be considered a crime.' Jimmy admits that he couldn't meet the demand from his customers, and that he certainly never needed to do any pushing. Darren adds that although he and Jimmy covered roughly the same territory in Ipswich they hadn't come across each other until they ended up in jail, which will give you an idea of just how large the market is.

Just in case you've forgotten, I'm still in the gym. Monster leaves me to join Darren and Jimmy on the bench press, where he manages to pump ten reps of 250 pounds. I also turn to the weights where I achieve ten curls at 50 pounds. This is followed by a spell on the bicycle, where I break the world record by peddling three miles in twelve minutes and fifty-four seconds. Pity it's the world record for running.

Mr Maiden, the senior gym instructor, reintroduces me to the medicine ball, which I haven't come in contact with since I left school. I place the large leather object behind my head, raise my shoulders as in an ordinary sit-up, and then pass it up to him. He then drops it back on top of me. Simple, I think, until I reach my fifth attempt, by which time I'm exhausted and Mr Maiden is unable to hide his mirth at my discomfort. He knows only too well that I haven't done this exercise for over forty years, and what the result would be.

'We'll have you doing three sets of fifteen with a minute interval between sets before you're released,' he promises.

'I hope not,' I tell him, without explanation. I then carry out a fifteen-minute warm down and stretching as my trainer in London (Karen) would have demanded. At the end of the session

SUNDAY 19 AUGUST 2001

I am first at the gate, because I'll have to be in and out of the shower fairly quickly if I'm to get to the library before the doors are locked.

10.21 am

Jog to my cell, strip, shower, change, jog to the library. Still sweating, but nothing I can do about it. Steve (conspiracy to murder) is on duty behind the desk in his position as chief librarian. Because Steve's the senior Listener, he's allowed to wear his own clothes and is often mistaken for a member of staff. I return *Famous Trials* and take out *Twenty-one Short Stories* by Graham Greene.

10.30 am

Once I've left the library I walk straight across the corridor to the chapel and discover there are thirty worshippers in the congregation this week. From their dress, the majority must come from the local village. The black man sitting next to me, who was among the seven prisoners who attended last week, tells me it's the biggest turnout he's ever seen. This week a Methodist minister called Mary conducts the service, accompanied by an Anglican vicar called Val. Mary's sermon is topical. She talks about the World Athletics Championships and her feelings for those competitors who did not achieve what they had set out to do, but for many of them there will be another chance. I have now attended four consecutive church services, and the minister always pitches the message at what he or she imagines will be of interest to the inmates. Each time they have failed to treat us as if we might just be normal human beings. People who have not been to prison tend to fall into two categories. The majority who treat you as if you're a 'convict on the run' while the minority treat you as if you are in their front room.

After the blessing, we gather in an ante-room for coffee and biscuits with the locals. No need to describe them as they don't differ greatly from the kind of parishioners who attend church services up and down the country every Sunday morning. Average age double that of the prisoners. At twelve we are sent back to our cells. No search. Unaccompanied.

12 noon

Lunch. I haven't had a chance to speak to Dale or Sergio yet, so I fix appointments with Dale at 2 pm and Sergio at 3 pm. I leave the hotplate with a portion of macaroni liberally covered in cheese.

While we are waiting in the long queue, Darren tells me when it used to be almost all macaroni with little sign of any cheese. Nobody thought to comment about this, until it became clear that the allocation of cheese was becoming smaller and smaller as each week passed. Still no one did anything about it, until one week, when there was virtually no cheese, the officer on duty at last began to show some interest. The first thing he discovered was that the same cook had been on for the previous four Saturdays and Sundays, so the following weekend he kept an eye on that particular inmate. He quickly discovered that on Saturday night the prisoner in question was returning to his cell with a lump of cheese the size of a pillow (5kg). It was when three loaves of bread also went missing the same evening that the officer decided to report the incident to the governor. The following Saturday night a team of officers raided the prisoner's cell hoping to find out what he was up to. They discovered that he was running a very successful business producing Welsh rarebit, which, when toasted, was passed from cell to cell through the bars of his little window.

'And damn good they were,' adds Jimmy, licking his lips.

'How did he manage to toast them?' I demanded.

'On every wing there is a communal iron, which always ended up in Mario's cell on a Saturday evening,' explained Darren.

'How much did the chef charge?'

'For two nights' supply, a two-pound phonecard.'

'And how did they punish him?'

'The iron was confiscated, and Mario demoted to washer-up, with twenty-one days added to his sentence. But they had to reinstate him after a couple of months because so many inmates complained about the standard of cooking dropping during the weekends. So he was brought back, and after another six months they also forgot about the twenty-one-day added sentence.

'And what is Mario in for?' I ask.

'Tax evasion – three years – and the fraud squad needed to be just as sharp to discover what he was up to then,' says Darren as we leave the hotplate. I make a mental note to make sure I meet him.

2.00 pm

Dale wants to talk to me about my canteen list for next week and has set an upper limit of £20. 'Otherwise the screws will become suspicious,' he explains. £20 will be quite enough as I'm still credited each week with £12.50 from my own account. Dale's also solved my writing pad problem, because he's some-how got his hands on three A4 pads, for which he charges me £4. I would happily pay £10 as I'm down to twenty pages of my last pad, but this new supply should last me a month.

DAY 32

5.00 pm

I call Mary at Grantchester, but there is no reply. I try London but only get Alison's voice on the answer machine. I forgot she's away on holiday. In any case, it's Sunday.

5.45 pm

Supper. The ham looks good, but I'm down for the vegetarian dish and you can't change your mind once you've signed the weekly menu sheet. Dale thinks about giving me a slice, but as my bête noire is on duty behind the hotplate, he doesn't risk it. Every Sunday you are given a meal sheet which rotates on a four-week cycle (see opposite); you fill in your selection from a list posted outside the main office, giving the kitchen advance notice of how much they will have to order of each item. Can't complain about that.

6.00 pm

Banged up for the next fourteen hours. I begin *The Basement Room* by Graham Greene. His description of minor characters is breathtaking in its simplicity and the story, although complex, still demands that you turn the page. I consider it a reflection on the Nobel Committee, not Mr Greene, that he has never won the prize for literature.

Ch. 2.

INMATE PRE-SELECT MENU SHEET							

CELL NO		NAME				NUMBER	
A2-49.		Archer				FF8282	

	MON	TUE	WED	THU	FRI	SAT	SUN
D	1	1	1	1	1	1	1
I	2	2	2	2	2	2	2
N	3	3	3	3	3	3	3
N	4	4	4	4	4	4	4
E	5	5	5	5	5	5	5
R	6	6	6	6	6		
	7	7	7	7	7		

	MON	TUE	WED	THU	FRI	SAT	SUN
T	1	1	1	1	1	1	1
	2	2	2	2	2	2	2
E	3	3	3	3	3	3	3
	4	4	4	4	4	4	4
A	5	5	5	5	5	5	5
	6	6	6	6	6	6	
	7	7	7	7	7	7	

WEEK NO: 9   DATE: AUGUST 19 2001

PLEASE CIRCLE ONE CHOICE FOR EACH MEAL FROM MENU AND
RETURN TO WING OFFICE BY WEDNESDAY LUNCH

INMATE'S SIGNATURE: Jeffrey Archer

cbs 6 February 1998

R3

DAY 33   MONDAY 20 AUGUST 2001

5.54 am

Wake and wonder how long it will take the police to close their file on the Kurds and allow me to be transferred to an open prison. I heard a story yesterday about a prisoner who wanted to do it the other way round. He put in an application to be transferred from a D-cat open prison to a C-cat – a more secure environment with a tougher regime. His reasons seem strange but, I'm told, are not uncommon.

He was serving a twenty-two-year sentence for murder. After five years, they moved him from an A-cat to a B-cat, which is a little more relaxed. After a further twelve years they transferred him to Wayland. At Wayland he became an enhanced prisoner with all the privileges that affords. He was also chief gardener, which allowed him to be out of his cell for most of the day and gave him an income of more than £30 a week. In his own world he wanted for nothing, and the governor considered him to be a model prisoner.

After twenty years he was granted D-cat status as part of his preparation for returning to the outside world. He was transferred to Ford Open Prison in Sussex to begin his rehabilitation.

He lasted at Ford for less than a month. One Saturday afternoon he absconded and turned himself in at the local police station a few hours later. He was arrested, charged with attempting to abscond and sent back to Wayland, where he remained until he had completed his sentence.*

The governor at the time couldn't resist asking him why he'd absconded. He replied that he couldn't handle the responsibility of making his own decisions. He also missed not having a proper job and the ordered discipline of the Wayland regime. But most of all he missed the high walls that surrounded the prison because they made him feel safe from all those people on the outside.

With less than six months to go before the end of his sentence, he was found in his cell with a piece of silver paper from a KitKat wrapper, a few grams of heroin and a lighted match.† He had even pressed the emergency button inside his cell to make certain that he was caught.

The governor wasn't sure what to do, because he knew only too well that the prisoner had never taken heroin in twenty years. Only six weeks were added to his sentence and he was released a few months later.

Within a month of leaving prison, he committed suicide.‡

---

* You can't escape from a D-cat, only abscond; a mistake the press continually make – because the word escape makes a better headline.

† The most ingenious method I came across for smoking heroin is to soak a Benson & Hedges packet in water and then separate the gold foil from the cardboard.

‡ Most suicides occur during the early stages of entering prison or soon after being released. Martin Narey, the Director General (now Commissioner for Correctional Services) spends a great deal of time telling the press how concerned he is about the number of suicides in prison – which incidentally have gone up every year during the past decade. What he doesn't tell you is how many suicides occur within a year of leaving prison, which is a far more damning indictment of the Prison Service's rehabilitation programme.

DAY 33

8.15 am

Breakfast. I have a Shredded Wheat and think of Ian Botham. This is doubly appropriate because it's twenty years ago this week that he scored 149 at Headingley and, with the assistance of Willis and Dilly, defeated Australia, despite England having to follow on. In today's match, Australia lead by 314, and I assume Adam Gilchrist will soon declare, as they've already won the series and England have only scored more than 300 in a final innings against Australia once in the last hundred years.

9.11 am

One of the prison chaplains visits me. She bears a message from Michael Adie, who until recently was the Bishop of Guildford. Michael and I first met in 1969 when he was Vicar of Louth and I was the Member of Parliament for that beautiful constituency.* He was a more natural friend for Mary, having gained a first-class honours degree in mathematics at Cambridge. Michael wants to visit me and has discovered that a bishop can see a prisoner without it affecting his quota of fortnightly visits.

I suggest to Margaret, the prison chaplain, that for Michael to make the long journey to Norfolk is typical of his generous spirit, but it might be wiser to wait and find out which D-cat prison they are going to transfer me to. I feel sure it will be nearer London and he could then visit me there. She kindly agrees to relay that message back to him.

---

* We sat in the House of Lords together, and his contributions on a range of subjects were formidable.

12 noon

Lunch. When I reach the hotplate, Dale looks anxious and whispers that he has to see me urgently.

I return to my cell, flick on the television to find that England are 12 for 2 and an Australian victory now looks certain. All we can hope for now is a draw. The untutored Jules thinks England can still win. Bless him. After all, he has only taken to watching cricket because he's stuck in the same cell as me.

2.00 pm

Gym. I complete my usual programme and feel I'm just about back to the level of fitness I was before being sentenced. I leave the exercise room to check up on what's happening in the main hall, where I find a volleyball match in progress. So many prisoners want to join in that they are playing one team on and one team off. By the end of the game, I accept the fact that I can no longer hope to play at this level, and appoint myself referee. Within a minute, I've given a penalty point because a prisoner swears following one of my decisions. A near riot breaks out and it's several minutes before I can get the game started again. What then follows is a close, well-fought match without another swear word uttered. When I blow the final whistle, the players on both sides all turn to face me, and swear as one.

3.20 pm

After a shower, I sit in my tiny cell and watch England fight their way back to 107 for 2. Jules is still convinced England can win. Dale visits me in my cell soon after Jules has disappeared off to education. Dale warns me that he's been interviewed by a security officer. Although they have no proof, they are fairly sure that the five £20 postal orders he received last week came from me, and they've warned him that if any further monies materialize that cannot be accounted for, they'll set up a full enquiry. We both agree that payments will have to cease, and with it my weekly supplies. Help!

3.50 pm

The same officer interviews me thirty minutes later, saying he has reason to believe I have been sending money in to another prisoner. The officer could not have been more reasonable, and adds that if it occurs again, it could greatly harm my chances of regaining D-cat status. It is then that he asks me if I am being bullied and paying someone to protect me. I burst out laughing. The officer obviously feels that Dale, at six foot three and twenty-seven stone, is my paid minder.

I make it clear that no one is bullying me, and I don't require any protection, but if I do he will be the first person to hear about it. The last thing I need is to jeopardize my D-cat, or be beaten up.

I return to my cell to find England are 207 for 3 at tea and Butcher is playing out of his skin. Even McGrath is being regularly dispatched to all parts of the ground. Could Jules be right?

4.30 pm

Exercise. I go out into the yard every day now, not just because I need the exercise but to pick up stories from the prisoners on different wings. Many of them are professional criminals, while others are just stupid or lazy. The most dangerous and frightening are a combination of all three. However, a minority are bright; but for the circumstances of their upbringing many of them might well have held down responsible positions. Darren agrees with me, but pointing to an inmate a few paces ahead of us, adds, 'But not in his case.'

'Why?' I ask. 'Who's he?'

'That's Dumbo,' he says, but offers no further explanation until we have passed him and he is well out of earshot.

'In December last year,' Darren continues, 'Dumbo was unemployed and facing the prospect of a distinctly un-merry Christmas. His wife said she'd had enough, and told him to go out and get some money and she didn't care how. Dumbo disappeared off to the town's largest toy store, where he shop-lifted a replica gun. He then walked across the road, held up the local chemist and departed with fourteen hundred pounds in cash. He returned home, handed over the money to his wife, confident that she would feel he'd done a good day's work. But after counting the notes, she told him that it wasn't enough and to go and get some more. Hold your breath,' said Darren, 'Dumbo once again leaves his home, returns to the high street, walks back into the same chemist shop with the intention of repeating the hold-up, only to find two police officers inter-viewing the proprietor. Dumbo was arrested on the spot, accom-panied to the nearest police station, charged and later sentenced to eight years for robbery while in the possession of a firearm.'

No novelist would dare to consider such a plot.

5.15 pm

When I return to my cell, Jules is glued to the television. Butcher is still at the crease. We both watch as Jules's prediction comes true and England sweep to a famous victory – Butcher, having scored the winning run, is 173 not out. This is an innings he will not be the only person to remember for the rest of his life.

I feel I should point out that Jules is every bit as excited as I am. A convert. A week ago he couldn't understand a draw, let alone what a follow on was, now he can't wait for next Thursday to watch the fifth and final test. I do hope he doesn't expect them all to end like this.

5.45 pm

Supper. I'm tucking into my beans and chips when Mr Meanwell unlocks the cell door and asks to have a private word with me. He doesn't speak again until we are in his office and the door is closed.

'You were lucky to have got away with it this time, but don't do it again,' he warns me. 'If you do, it could hold up your D-cat for months. And if you're thinking of doing anything with Sergio, wait until he's completed his sentence.' I'm impressed by how well-informed Mr Meanwell is.*

---

* Most officers cultivate their own informers, but do not reveal to anyone, including other officers, who they are.

DAY 34   TUESDAY 21 AUGUST 2001

6.11 am

Slept well, write for two hours.

8.15 am

Breakfast. It's Rice Crispies again. It's taken me until the middle of the second week to work out that it's Shredded Wheat on Monday, Rice Crispies on Tuesday, cornflakes on Wednesday. Nothing changes. Everything is by rote.

10.00 am

My induction seems to have run its course. However, I remain on the induction wing as I wait for a single cell to become vacant. I am made aware of this because the cycle has begun again: a new group of prisoners is being seen by a member of the Board of Visitors. I peer through the little mesh window in the door; it's not Mr Flintcroft this time, but a lookalike.

DAY 34

10.15 am

Education. I pull on my newly supplied prison regulation heavy brown boots as I prepare for my first pottery lesson. Once I've left the spur I have to ask several officers and inmates the way to the Art Centre, which turns out to be on the other side of the prison.

When I finally locate it, the first person I see on entering the room is Shaun, who sits in the corner of the large square workshop working on an abstract pastel. He greets me with a smile. The next person I spot is a lady who I assume must be our tutor. She's around five foot six, dark-haired and dark-eyed with a warm smile. She introduces herself as Anne.

The first task Anne sets me is to read a pottery book and see if I come across any object I'd like to recreate. I try to tell her about my lack of talent in this area, but she just smiles. I begin to read the book as she moves on to Roger, a jolly West Indian (bank robber), who is doing a sculpture of the Virgin Mary. She then goes across to Terry (burglar), who is moulding his piece of clay into a lion. I am engrossed in my book when Anne returns, accompanied by a large lump of clay. She also has a thin wooden stick that looks like a knife without a handle, which is numbered four. She glances down at the page I've reached to see a head and shoulders figure of a man. With the help of the wooden knife, she carves chunks off the square putty to start forming the shoulders, and then leaves me to begin my first attempt at figurative sculpture.

As I turn my attention to the head and neck, I get into conversation with Shaun who is rubbing his fingers into the pastel to try and give his picture a blurred 'Turneresque' look. While he chats away about which artists influence him, I subtly try to steer the conversation off art and find out why he is in prison, quite expecting him to claim that he's another victim of drugs.

'No, no, no,' he says. 'Forgery.' My ears prick up.

'Paintings?' I ask.

'No,' he replies. 'Much as I'd like to be a Keating or Elmyr Hory, it's more mundane than that – John Lewis gift vouchers.'

I laugh. 'So how were you caught?'

'I was grassed up by my mate who got nervous and turned Queen's evidence. He got off while I ended up with thirteen months in prison.'

'Thirteen months? That's a strange sentence.'

'I was given twelve months for the forgery and an extra month for not turning up to the first hearing.'

'How much did you get away with?' I ask casually.

'Can't tell you that,' he responds. 'But I admitted to a couple of grand.'

'And you'll be out in three weeks, so how long have you served?'

'Just over four months.'

'So you haven't that long to carry out my commission.'

He turns back to his sketch pad and flicks over a few pages. He reveals half a dozen sketches of five figures in different poses and asks which one I would prefer.

'Which one do *you* prefer?'

'Number three,' he says, placing his thumb on the sketch (see plate section). I nod my agreement as Anne reappears by my side.

'I see what you mean by lack of talent,' she says, and bursts out laughing at my feeble effort of a head and shoulders, which looks like a cross between ET and a Botero. Roger (bank robber) and Terry (burglar) come across to find out what's causing such merriment.

'You should have started with a pot, man,' says Roger, 'and not tried to advance so quickly.' He's already identified my biggest failing.

Without warning, two officers march in and begin to carry out a search. I assume it must be to check on the number of wooden knives and wire used for slicing the putty. But no, I'm told later it was for drugs. The workshops are evidently a common place for dealers to conduct their business.

On the way back to my cell I get lost again, but Shaun accompanies me to A wing and tells me that he has come up with a concept for the cover of *Wayland* (see plate section). I had always assumed that a graphic designer would do the cover of the book, but the idea of a fellow prisoner carrying out the commission is very appealing. I also admire Shaun's enterprise in spotting the opportunity. As we part at the T-junction between our two blocks, we agree to meet up during afternoon exercise to continue the discussion.

12 noon

Lunch. Dale's mushroom soup plus a vegetable fritter.

2.14 pm

I call my solicitor to try to find out the latest on the Simple Truth investigation. The police have been supplied with all our documents plus a detailed report from the Red Cross. Detective Chief Superintendent Perry, who's in charge of the case, is sympathetic, but says he must follow up all Baroness Nicholson's accusations. To DCS Perry a day is nothing; to me it's another fourteen hours locked in a cell.

5.00 pm

Supper: Chinese stir-fry and vegetables. An original recipe served up in one blob, and certainly not cooked by anyone who originated from the Orient.

6.00 pm

No evening gym because there is a cricket match between A and D blocks (the drug-free wing known as junkies' paradise).* I am going over my script for the day when Jimmy appears outside my cell door.

'You're batting at number five, my lord,' he says, looking down at his team sheet.

'What?' I say. 'The last game I played was for David Frost's eleven against the Lords Taverners and on that occasion I was clean bowled first ball.'

'Who was the bowler?' he asks.

'Imran Khan,' I reply.

'The Pakistani fast bowler?' he asks in disbelief.

'Yes, but he was bowling slow leg breaks at the time.'

'You're still batting number five. Report to the top corridor in five minutes.'

I change into a tracksuit, place a bottle top in the gap in my door† and run to the gate to find Darren waiting for me.

'Like the new Swatch,' he says. 'What happened to the Longines?'

---

* Many prisoners ask to go on the 'drug-free block' as it helps with their chances of early parole, while having no intention of coming off drugs.
† If you put a Robinsons bottle top in the gap where the bolt goes, you can leave your cell, push the door to, and it appears closed. When you return, you can pull it open without having to bother an officer. The officers turn a blind eye to this subterfuge – for obvious reasons.

I tell him of my illicit transfer of the watch to Will during the last family visit.

'The screws will have spotted it,' Darren assures me, 'and they would have been only too happy to see that particular watch leave the prison. Think of the trouble it would have caused them if someone had stolen it. Be warned, they don't miss much.'

'By the way,' adds Darren, 'one of the guys on our wing is being transferred tomorrow, so this may be your chance to get off the induction spur.'

My heart leaps at the news. I try to find out more details as we continue our stroll through a gate and out onto a large open field that is surrounded by a high fence topped with razor wire.*

Jimmy wins the toss and elects to bat. Now, for those of you who understand the game of cricket, HM prisons keep to a set of laws that even the MCC have no jurisdiction over. They may or may not give you a better insight into prison thinking:

(a) Both sides have ten overs each.

(b) Each over is nine balls and you never change ends.

(c) Each side must play five bowlers who can bowl two overs each, but not consecutively.

(d) There are no boundaries and you have to run every run.

(e) The side with the highest score is the winner.

(f) The umpire's decision is final.

While the other side takes to the field, Dale and Carl pad up for A block. I look in the equipment trolley, hoping I will find a box and a helmet. At the age of sixty-one I don't fancy facing a twenty-two-year-old West Indian bowler from Brixton who thinks it would be fun to put me in hospital with no fear of

---

* The use of razor wire is another example of the Prison Service breaking European law, preferring to pay a hefty fine each year.

being arrested for it. I can't believe my eyes: bats, pads, helmets, guards, boxes and gloves that are far superior to anything I've ever seen at any club game.

Our openers are both back in the pavilion by the end of the first over with the score at 6 for 2. We may well have first-class equipment, but I quickly discover that it does little for our standard of cricket. Our number four lasts for three balls so in the middle of the third over I find myself walking out to join Jimmy.

D Block boo me all the way to the crease, bringing a new meaning to the word 'sledging'. However, there is worse to come because the West Indian I referred to earlier is licking his lips in anticipation. Hell, he's fast, but he's so determined to kill me that accuracy is sacrificed and his nine-ball over is extended to thirteen, with four wides. After another couple of overs (don't forget, nine balls each), Jimmy and I advance happily on to 35 for 4. That is when my captain decides to try and launch the ball over the prison fence and ends up having his middle stump removed.

I fear neither Neville Cardus nor E. W. Swanton could have done justice to our progress from 35 for 4 to 39 all out. All you need to know is that the West Indian is back on for his second over, and during the next nine balls he takes five wickets at a cost of four runs. I leave the pitch 11 not out, having not faced a ball since my captain returned to the pavilion (bowlers don't change ends). But all is not lost because when A block takes to the field – thanks to our demon quickie Vincent (manslaughter) – three of our opponents are back in the pavilion by the end of the first over, for a total of only five runs.

The second bowler is *our* West Indian. He is robbed with two dropped catches and a plump LBW, or I felt so from cover point. When he comes off, D block have only reached 9 for 2, but then prison rules demand that we render up our third bowler. On his arrival, the game is quickly terminated as the ball is peppered ruthlessly around the pitch. D block reach the required total with no further loss of wickets and five overs to spare.

On the way back to our cells, the D block captain says, 'Not bad, Jeff, even though you played like a fucking public school cunt.' In prison you have to prove yourself every day.

Once we're back inside the block, I tell Jimmy that I may be joining him on the enhanced spur.

'I don't think so, Jeff,' he replies. 'The man who's leaving us is our wing cleaner, and I think they've offered his cell to David (whisky bootlegger), the cleaner on your wing.' My heart sinks. 'Your best bet is to move into David's cell, and stay there until another one comes free.'

8.00 pm

I return to my cell, but unfortunately there's no time for a shower before we're all banged up. I'm tired, sweaty, and even aching a little, having used muscles I don't normally press into action in the gym. I'm also hungry, so I open a tin of Princes ham (49p) and a packet of crisps (27p).

9.00 pm

Jules watches *The Bill*, while I continue to read Graham Greene's *The Man Within*. I fall asleep wondering if this is to be my last night in a double cell.

DAY 35   WEDNESDAY 22 AUGUST 2001

6.04 am

Wake. Fantasize about the possibility of a single cell. Write for two hours.

8.15 am

Breakfast. Cornflakes and one slice of toast. Dale is missing from behind the hotplate.

8.40 am

Spot Dale in the corridor. He tells me he's resigned from his job on the hotplate. He's sick of getting up thirty minutes before the rest of us just to be abused by inmates who never feel their portion of chips is large enough.

I see my name is chalked up on the blackboard outside the main office to report to the SO, Mr Meanwell. I go straight to the office. He has a registered letter for me, and slits it open. He extracts a two-sided typed missive which he hands over, but shows no interest in reading. While he checks inside the envelope for drugs, money, even stamps, I begin to read the letter, and after only a paragraph, pass it back to Mr Meanwell. When he peruses it, a look of disbelief comes over his face. The writer wants to borrow £10,000 to invest in 'an impossible to lose deal' and he's willing to split the profits fifty–fifty.

'How often do you get one of these?' he asks.

'Two or three times a week,' I confess, 'asking for sums for as little as fifty pounds right up to a million for yet another "impossible to lose deal".'

'By the way,' he says as he hands me the empty envelope, 'you may be moving today.' By the way, by the way, by the way – so casual for him, so important to me. 'One of the chaps on the enhanced spur is being transferred to a prison nearer his home and we're allocating his cell to an inmate who will take over his responsibilities as cleaner. Once that's been sorted out,' – Mr Meanwell is old enough still to include the word 'out' – 'we'll move you into his cell. I did think of sending you straight to the enhanced spur,' he admits, 'but there were two reasons not to. First, the spur needs a cleaner and you wouldn't be my first choice for that particular job, and second, I want you on the quieter side where it's not possible for other prisoners to peer through your window during exercise.'

Once I leave Mr Meanwell, I go in search of David (whisky bootlegger and spur cleaner). I find him attached to the industrial cleaner whirring around the floor of the induction corridor. He invites me along to his present cell on the first floor which, compared to my one up, one down on the induction wing, is the difference between Fawlty Towers and the Ritz.

11.00 am

Exercise. During the first circuit I'm asked by Chris (burglary) if I'll sponsor him for a half marathon in aid of the NSPCC. I agree to £1 a mile, as long as it comes out of my private finances and not my canteen account. Otherwise I'll be without food and bottled water for several weeks. He assures me that the authorities will allow that, so I sign up. He sticks with us for half a circuit, by which time I've learnt that he's the type of burglar our probation officer, Lisa Dada, so despises. He's twenty-seven years old and has spent eight of the last ten years in jail. He simply considers burglary a way of life. In fact, his parting words are, 'I'm out in six weeks' time, Jeff, but don't worry, your house is safe.' I realize those of you who have never been to jail may find this strange, but I now feel more sympathy for some of the murderers in Belmarsh than I do for professional burglars.

It was sometime later that I began to ponder on how he could run thirteen miles without occupying half the local constabulary to make sure he didn't escape. I'll ask him tomorrow.

Jason (conspiracy to blackmail) joins us on the second circuit and congratulates me on being moved to a single cell.

'It hasn't happened yet,' I remind him.

'No, but it will this afternoon.'

Prison has many similarities to the outside world. One is that you quickly discover who actually knows what's going on and who only picks up fag ends. Jason knows exactly what's happening.

'Of course, if you want to,' Jason adds, 'you can always get yourself transferred to another prison.'

'And how would I manage that?'

'Write yourself a note and drop it in the complaints box. You don't even have to sign it. It's known as "the grass box".'

'And what would I have to suggest?'

'Archer is offering me drugs and I can't resist much longer, or Archer is bullying me and I'm near breaking point. If they believe it, you'd be transferred the same day. In fact your feet wouldn't even touch the ground.'

12 noon

Lunch. The hotplate seems empty without the massive frame of Dale dominating proceedings. It looks as if Sergio has been promoted to No. 1 in his place, because he now stands next to the duty officer and hands out the dishes according to whether you're one, two, three (vegetarian) or four.

'Three,' Sergio says, without even glancing at the list, and then carefully selects my dish. The transfer of power has in no way affected me.

1.45 pm

Gym. The treadmill is working again so I'm almost able to carry out a full programme. With the new medicine ball exercise I'm up to fifteen, with a one-minute break, but after a further nine I'm exhausted and grateful when Mr Maiden blows the five-minute whistle so I can warm down. As we leave, everyone else picks up their assigned gym card before disappearing back to their cells. I no longer have a gym card. It's been stolen every day since I arrived, and the management have given up bothering to issue me with a new one.

3.30 pm

I come out of the shower to find Ms Webb waiting for me.

'When the induction wing is banged up at four o'clock,' she says, 'I'll leave your door open because we're going to move you across to number two cell on the far spur.'

I think about throwing my arms round Ms Webb, but as I only have a towel covering me, I feel sure she would put me on report, so I simply say, 'Thank you.'

Once I'm dressed, I place all my belongings into the Belmarsh plastic bag in preparation for the move to the other side of the block. I am packed and ready to leave long before four.

This will be my eighth move in five weeks.

4.06 pm

David (whisky bootlegger) is waiting for me in his old cell. It's typical of his good manners that he has left the room spotless. Now that I have an extra cupboard, it takes me nearly an hour to decide where everything should go. Although the cell remains the regulation five paces by three, it suddenly feels much larger when you no longer have to share the cramped space with another prisoner. No more having to keep out of someone else's way. No more television programmes I don't want to watch. No more having to check whose slippers you've put on, that you're using your own toothpaste, soap, even lavatory paper. No more ... There's a knock on the cell door and Darren, Jimmy, Sergio and Steve make an entrance.

'It's a house-warming party,' Darren explains, 'and, like any good party, we come bearing gifts.'

Sergio has three five-by-five-inch steel mirrors, the regulation size. He fixes them on the wall with prison toothpaste. I can now see my head and upper body for the first time in five weeks. Steve supplies – can you believe it – net curtains to hide my barred window, and at night tone down the glare of the fluorescent lights. Jimmy has brought all the paraphernalia needed – board, Blu-tack, etc. – to attach my family photos to the wall. And Darren demands a roll of drums before he will reveal his gift, because he's come up with every prisoner's dream: a plug. No longer will I have to shave in my cereal bowl.

'Anything else you require, my lord?' Steve enquires.

'I'm out of Evian.'

For the first time the visiting team admits defeat. A survey has been carried out and it's been discovered that I am the only prisoner on the block who purchases bottled water from the canteen.

'So, like the rest of us,' says Darren, 'if you want more water, you'll have to turn on the tap.'

'However,' adds Sergio, 'now that I'm number one on the hotplate,' he pauses, 'you will be able to have an extra carton of milk from time to time.'

What more could a man ask for?

7.00 pm

I read over today's script in my silent cell and when I've finished editing I place the six pages in one of my new drawers. Every ten days the sheets are transferred to a large brown envelope (30,000 words) and sent off to Alison to type up.

I settle down on my bed to watch *A Touch of Frost*. David Jason is as consistent as ever, but the script is too flimsy to sustain itself for two hours, so I switch off the television and, for the first time in ten days, also the light, climb into my single bed and sleep. Goodbye, window warriors, may I never hear from you again.

DAY 36   THURSDAY 23 AUGUST 2001

5.18 am

I wake, depressed about two matters. When I phoned Mary last night, she told me that the Red Cross have asked KPMG to audit the Simple Truth campaign, because some of their larger donors have been making waves and they want to close the subject once and for all. Tony Morton-Hooper wrote to the police, pointing out that this internal audit has nothing to do with my involvement with the campaign. Mary and Tony are doing everything they can to get the police to admit that the whole enquiry is a farce and that Ms Nicholson's accusations were made without a shred of evidence. Despite their efforts I have a feeling the police will not close their enquiry until they've considered his report, so it could now be months before my D-cat is reinstated.

I'm also depressed because the Tory party seems to have broken out into civil war, with Margaret Thatcher saying it will be a disaster if Ken Clarke wins, and John Major declaring that if IDS becomes leader we'll be in Opposition for another decade. Six years so far.

DAY 36

6.00 am

I write for two hours.

8.15 am

After breakfast, Darren picks up my laundry, and warns me that the tumble dryer is still not functioning.

9.00 am

Banged up for another two hours because the staff are having their fortnightly training session in the gym. I'm told their activities range from first-aid lessons to self-defence (secure and protect), from checking through the latest Home Office regulations to any race relations problems, plus fire training, HIV reports and likely suicide candidates. One good thing about all this is that the tax payer is saved having to fund my pottery class (£1.20).

11.00 am

I watch Nassar Hussain lose the toss for the fourteenth time in a row. I must ask Mary what the odds are against that.*

I walk out into the exercise yard just before the gates are closed at five past eleven. Jimmy points to Mario (not his real name) who is walking a few paces ahead of us. I hope you can recall Mario's scam. While working on the hotplate he stole almost all the cheese. He then made Welsh rarebit, at a phone-card for two, using an iron as the toaster. Mario was caught

_____

* Mary tells me they are 1 in 2 to the power of 14, which is 1 in 16,384.

creaming off nearly half a million a year from his fashionable London restaurant without bothering to pay any tax on his windfall. Although I have never frequented Mario's establishment, I know it by reputation. There can be no doubt of the restaurant's success, because it was one of those rare places that do not accept credit cards – only cash or cheques.

While we stroll round the yard – Mario's not into power walking – he explains that approximately half of his income was in cash, the rest cheques or accounts. However, the taxman had no way of finding out what actual percentage was cash, until two tax inspectors visited the restaurant as diners. From careful observation they concluded that nearly half the customers were paying cash, whereas Mario's tax return showed a mere 10 per cent settled the bill this way. But how could they prove it? The inspectors paid cash themselves and requested a receipt. What they couldn't know was that Mario declared all the bills where the customer asked for a receipt, which he then entered in his books. Bills for which no receipts were given were destroyed and the cash then pocketed.

The taxmen couldn't become regular customers (their masters wouldn't allow such an extravagance) and were therefore unable to prove any wrongdoing. That was until a young, newly qualified accountant joined the Inland Revenue and came up with an ingenious idea as to how to ensnare Mario. The fresh-faced youth found out which laundry the restaurant used and over the next three months had the tablecloths and napkins counted. There were 40 per cent more tablecloths than bills and 38 per cent more napkins than customers.

Mario was arrested and charged with falsifying his accounts. He pleaded guilty and was sentenced to two years. He will be returning to his restaurant later this year having, in answer to customers' enquiries, taken a 'sabbatical' in his native Florence.

DAY 36

'They've got it all wrong, Jeffrey,' Mario says. 'The likes of you and me shouldn't be in jail mixing with all this riff-raff. They should have fined me a million pounds, not paid out thirty-five thousand to accommodate me for a year. My regulars are livid with the police, the courts and the Inland Revenue.' His final words are, 'By the way, Jeffrey, do you like buck rarebit?'

12 noon

Lunch. Among the many things Mario briefed me on was how to select the best daily dish from the weekly menu. You must only choose dishes that are made with fresh ingredients grown on the premises and not bought in. As from next week there will be variations from my usual vegetarian fare.

2.00 pm

I read the morning papers. Margaret and John have placed their cutlasses back in their sheaths and both have fallen silent – for the time being. The press are describing the leadership contest as the most acrimonious in living memory, and one from which the party may never recover. Reading this page a couple of years after the event will give us all the benefit of hindsight. Is it possible that the party that governed for the longest period of time during the twentieth century will not hold office in the twenty-first? Or will Tony Blair suddenly look fallible?

3.15 pm

Gym. It's the over-fifties' spinning session – nothing to do with politics. Don't kid yourself – it's agony. Forty-five minutes with an instructor shouting, 'On the straight', 'Up the slope', 'Hill climbing', 'Faster, faster'. I fall off the bike at four o'clock and Darren almost carries me back to my cell.

5.30 pm

Australia are 208 for 1 and looking as if they could score 700. I leave the cricket to get some loo paper from the store. This must be collected between 8.15–8.30 am or 5.30–6.00 pm; one roll per person, per week. As I come out of the store room, I notice my name is chalked up on the blackboard to see the SO. I go straight to Mr Meanwell's office. He has several registered letters for me, including one from some ladies in Northampton, who have sent me a lavender cake.

'I'm afraid you're not allowed to have it until you move prisons or have completed your sentence,' Mr Meanwell explains.

'Why not?' I ask.

'It could be laced with alcohol or drugs,' he tells me.

As I leave the SO's office, I spot a new prisoner with his right arm in a sling. I go over to have a chat: injuries usually mean stories. Was he in a fight? Was he hit by a prison officer? Did he fall or was he pushed? It turns out to be an attempted suicide. He shows me his wrist which displays three long, jagged scars forming a triangle which have been sewn up like a rough tear in a Turkish carpet. I stare for about a second at the crude, mauve scars before I have to turn away. Later, I'm relieved to discover that Jimmy reacted in the same way, though he tells me that if you really want to kill yourself, you don't cut across the artery.

'You only do that when you're looking for sympathy,' he adds, 'because the screws will always get there in time. But one long slash up the arm will sever the artery, and you'll die long before they can reach you.'

'Nevertheless,' I say, 'that's some cry for help.'

'Yes, his father had a heart attack last week, and he's just arrived back from the funeral.'

'How many suicides have there been at Wayland while you've been here?' I ask Jimmy.

'There was one about six weeks ago,' he replies. 'You'll always know when one takes place because we're banged up for the rest of the day. No one is allowed to leave their cell until the body has been removed from the prison. Then an initial report has to be written, and because so many officers become involved, including the governor, it never takes less than three hours. This prison's pretty good,' he adds. 'We only get about one suicide a year. In Norwich, where I began my sentence, it was far higher, more like one a month. We even had a prisoner sitting up on the roof with a noose round his neck, saying he'd jump unless the governor dealt with his complaint.'

'Did he jump?'

'No, they gave in and agreed to let him attend his mother's funeral.'

'But why didn't they agree to that in the first place?'

'Because last time they let him out, he flattened a screw with one punch and tried to escape.'

'So the governor gave in?'

'No, the governor refused to see him, but he did allow the prisoner to attend the funeral, double-cuffed.'

'Double-cuffed?'

'First they cross the prisoner's wrists before handcuffing him. Then they handcuff him to two officers with two separate pairs of handcuffs, one on either side.'

Thank God they didn't do that to me when I attended my mother's funeral.

It's an irony that an hour later, when going through my mail, I find a razor-blade paper attached to the top of one of my letters, with the message 'Just in case you've had enough.' The blade itself had been removed by an officer.

6.00 pm

Exercise. Shaun (forgery) has begun to work on an outline drawing of the montage. His first model is Dale (wounding with intent), who is standing on the grass in the sun, arms folded – not a natural model (see plate section). Dale scowls as we pass him, while a few of the other prisoners shout obscenities.

8.00 pm

Nothing worth watching on television, so I finish Graham Greene's *The Man Within*.

10.00 pm

I remove the newly washed clothes from all over my bed, where I had laid them out to dry. They are still wet so I hang them from every other available space – cupboard doors, the sink, my chair, even the curtain rail.

I fall asleep, still worrying about the KPMG report and how long it will take for the police to agree that there is no case to answer. By the time you read this, Wayland will be a thing of the past. But for now, it remains purgatory.

DAY 37   FRIDAY 24 AUGUST 2001

6.08 am

I draw my newly acquired curtains to allow the rising sun to enter my cell. I discovered during exercise yesterday evening that they used to belong to Dennis (VAT fraud). No one knows how much of the 17.5 per cent he retained for himself, but as he was sentenced to six years, we have to assume it was several millions.

Dennis applied for parole after two and a half years, having been a model prisoner. He heard nothing, so assumed that his request had been turned down. Yesterday, at 8 am, they opened his cell door and told him to pack his belongings. He was being released within the hour. The order had come from the Home Office the week before but, as his probation officer was on leave, no message had got through. Dennis had to borrow a phonecard – against prison regulations – to ask his wife to come and pick him up. He caught her just as she was leaving for work, otherwise he would have been standing outside the gates all day. That is how I inherited the fine net curtains which now adorn my cell, and when I leave they will be passed on to the new resident. I just hope I'm given a little more notice.

Jimmy was also let out yesterday, but only for the day. He

has just a few weeks left to serve before his release date, so they allow him out once a month on a town visit, from 9 am to 3 pm. This is part of the rehabilitation programme for any D-cat prisoner. Jimmy has been a D-cat, but resident in a C-cat prison, for over three months. He doesn't want to move to an open prison because he's coming to the end of his sentence and his family lives locally.

Yesterday Jimmy visited Dereham. He was accompanied by an officer who, for reasons that will become clear, I shall not name. At lunchtime the officer gave Jimmy a fiver to buy them both some fish and chips (Dereham prices) while he went to the bank to cash a cheque. Jimmy collected the fish and chips, strolled over to the National Westminster and waited outside for the officer. When he didn't appear, Jimmy began lunch without him. After the last chip had been devoured, Jimmy began to worry about what had happened to his guard. He went into the bank, but couldn't see him, so ran out and quickly headed towards Lloyds TSB, a hundred yards away. As he turned the corner, he saw the officer running down the street towards him, an anxious look on his face. The two men fell into each other's arms laughing; Jimmy didn't want to be accused of trying to escape only six weeks before his release date, and the officer would have been sacked for giving a prisoner money to assist in that escape. Jimmy told me later that he's never seen a more relieved man in his life.

'Where are my fish and chips?' demanded the officer, once he had recovered.

'I had to eat them, guv,' Jimmy explained, 'otherwise yours would have gone cold.' He handed over fifty pence change.

DAY 37

8.00 am

After breakfast I go in search of Stan (embezzler, £21,000, eighteen months), the spur painter. I ask him if he'd be kind enough to come and look at my cell and see if he can recommend any way of brightening it up. I tell him I hate the white door and the black square around the basin and the black floor skirting.

'I'll see what I can do,' he says, 'but I can't promise much. We only get colours that have been discontinued, or the ones no one else wants.'

9.00 am

Pottery. I fear this enterprise has proved to be a mistake. I simply don't have any talent with clay. I'm going to ask Wendy if I can be transferred to the library or education. The *Sun* told its readers yesterday that I had applied to take Dennis's (of curtain fame) job in the library. I didn't even know he worked in the library, but now the *Sun* has put the idea in my head, I'll ask Steve (conspiring to murder, head librarian) if there's a vacancy. Meanwhile I go off to pottery and waste two hours talking to Shaun (forgery). To be fair, it wasn't a complete waste of time because he brought me up to date on his progress with the book cover and the montage of prisoners (see plate section). I also discover more about his crime.

What I hadn't appreciated was that the forged John Lewis gift vouchers were not used simply to purchase articles from the store. Oh, no, Shaun is far brighter than that. He discovered that if you buy an item and present your gift voucher, the assistant will hand back the change in cash. Shaun also found out that if you purchase something for £1,000 (and he saw Chris Eubank buying a television with genuine vouchers) and return the item an hour later, they don't reimburse you with vouchers. Once again, they hand over cash.

Armed with this information, Shaun acquired a map of England (kindly supplied by a helpful assistant) showing every John Lewis outlet in the country. He then began to travel the land, cashing vouchers in each town he passed through. He was finally caught when his co-conspirator panicked, went to the police and grassed on him (Shaun's words).

I wonder what Shaun will turn his mind to once he's released. I only mention this because when the conversation changed to the clash between Ken Clarke and Iain Duncan Smith, Shaun added a piece of knowledge to the euro debate which neither of the candidates seems to have grasped.

'Have you ever seen a euro note?' Shaun asked.

'No, I haven't,' I admitted.

'It's Monopoly money and will be quite easy to reproduce. From 1 January it will be legal tender in seventeen countries across Europe, and I'll bet most of the shops don't have any way of identifying a fake. Someone's going to make a fortune.'

I recall that Shaun has only three more weeks of his sentence to serve.

11.15 am

I return to my cell and find I have a beige door, a neat blue square around my basin and cream skirting. I go in search of Stan, and present him with a phonecard – value: £2; worth: inestimable.

DAY 37

11.30 am

I call Paula (Alison is on holiday) and discover to my great relief
that the last ten days' text of this script have arrived. It doesn't
bear thinking about having to rewrite those 30,000 words. You
may well ask why I didn't make a copy. Because there isn't a
copier available. Then why don't I hand the papers over to my
wife after a visit? Because it's against the regulations. My only
chance is to rely on the Post Office, and it hasn't let me down
yet.

12 noon

Lunch. I mournfully watch the test match while eating my
vegetable soup. Australia are piling on the runs at a rate of four
an over.

3.00 pm

Exercise. Jimmy is chatting about his girlfriends, and don't forget
this is a man who had three women come to see him at his last
visit. At some time, he tells me, he's slept with all three of them
– not at the same time, he's not kinky, just healthy – and what's
more they didn't leave scratching each other's eyes out. Nevertheless, this brings me on to a taboo subject I haven't yet
mentioned: sex or the lack of it – unless you are a homosexual.
Darren reminds us that in Sweden and Holland they allow
conjugal visits, which I can't see happening in this country for
many years. The current solution is to put a notice on the
message board (see opposite) and hope the problem will go
away. It will be interesting to see which comes first: the legaliza-
tion of cannabis or conjugal visits.

After two weeks of walking round the perimeter of Wayland

HM PRISON SERVICE

HMP Wayland

OFFENSIVE AND OBSCENE MATERIAL

STATEMENT OF POLICY

1. At HMP Wayland we feel that it is important that we provide an environment within which visitors, staff and prisoners are able to work and visit without being caused offence by the display of any material.

2. Our aim is to ensure that the dignity of all staff, visitors and prisoners is respected. It is the duty of all staff to help to ensure that our environment remains free from the display of potentially offensive material.

3. Therefore the public display of any material that is potentially offensive will not be permitted in any part of the Prison.

TYPES OF MATERIAL THAT WILL BE RESTRICTED:

4. Any sexually explicit material, eg magazines of a pornographic nature which are available from newsagents, will be allowed in possession but must not be on display.

5. "Page 3" type pictures can be placed on prisoners' noticeboards, but pictures showing full nudity cannot. Photographs, artwork and other material may be displayed on noticeboards providing it conforms to the criteria outlined above.

6. All managers have a duty to ensure that their areas remain free from the display of any potentially offensive material. This applies to all areas, including offices, rest rooms and other "staff only" areas.

prison, I can now spot evil, fear, helplessness and sadness at thirty paces. But even I am puzzled by a crouching man who always sits alone in the same place every day, huddled up against the fence. He can't be much more than thirty, perhaps thirty-five, and he rarely moves from his solitary position. I ask Darren about him.

'Tragic,' he says. 'Alistair is one of your lot – public school, followed by university, where he graduated as a heroin addict. If he doesn't kick the habit, he'll be in prison for the rest of his life.'

'How can that be possible?' I ask.

'Simple. He regularly gets caught injecting himself, and always ends up with a few more months being added to his sentence. In fact, even on the day he was sent down, he was found with a needle in his arm. Somehow, and it must have been before the judge passed sentence or soon after he was taken down, he managed to stuff a needle covered in cellophane, a plunger and ten grams of heroin wrapped in a condom up his backside. He then took a laxative so that he could empty his bowels as soon as he arrived at Belmarsh. Once they'd banged him up that evening – and don't forget there's a lavatory in every cell – he injected himself with heroin and passed out. At the nine o'clock flap check* the night officer found him lying on the floor with a needle stuck in his arm and several grams of heroin sprinkled on the floor beside him. He must be one of the few prisoners who has managed to have time added to his sentence before breakfast the following morning.'

I look at the tragic, hunched-up figure and wonder if prison is the right answer.

---

* A flap check is when the duty officer makes sure you are in your cell and have not escaped.

6.00 pm

Supper. I can't remember what I eat, but I do recall finding two extra cartons of milk on my window sill. Sergio is exercising his authority as the new No. 1 on the hotplate.

DAY 38   SATURDAY 25 AUGUST 2001

5.11 am

I wake and think about how I would be spending the August bank holiday weekend if I were not in prison. I also begin to consider whether there are any advantages to being in jail. Certainly, incarceration is something to be added to one's experiences, particularly as it has come at a period in life when I felt I was marking time. I've also had to stretch myself – unfortunate pun. But I've already reached a stage where I am gaining little from the experience. As I could be stuck here for a while longer, it might be wise to have an escape plan – escape of the mind.

I've already completed *Belmarsh: Hell*, and have penned 44,000 words of *Wayland: Purgatory*. I can't wait to get to heaven, whenever and wherever that might be.

8.15 am

'*Buenos días,*' I say to Sergio as he passes me a boiled egg and a slice of toast.

'*Buenos días,*' he repeats. '*Cómo estas tú?*'

I concentrate. '*Yo estoy bien, gracias.*'

'*Bien, gracias, y tú?*'

'*Bien, gracias, y to?*'

'*No, tú, tú, tú.*'

'*Tú, tú, tú.*'

'*Bueno*. We must meet later today,' Sergio adds, 'for another lesson.' At least ten prisoners standing in the queue, and three officers behind the hotplate, assume I am simply learning Spanish, as we have no wish for them to find out what we're really up to. But more of that later.

10.00 am

Gym. I complete a full programme for the first time since being convicted. I've lost over half a stone and feel a lot fitter. I'm about to take a shower when Mr King tells me that the governor wants a word. I've so far seen three people who claim the title of governor, and none of them has been Ms Cawley, the No. 1 governor. Am I about to meet her? No. On this occasion it's a Mr Greenacre, whom I've also never come across before. He informs me, 'You will be receiving a visit from a senior officer at Belmarsh' – surely they can't be sending me back there, is my first reaction – 'as they are investigating the theft of a chapter of your book.' You will recall that Trevor Kavanagh of the *Sun*, doyen of political editors, returned those stolen seven pages to Mary. He is well aware of the law of copyright.

It is clear that the culprit must have been an officer as no prisoners at Belmarsh have access to a photocopier. No one else could have unlocked my cell door, removed the script, photocopied and returned it and then sent a copy on to the *Sun*.

Of course, the deputy governor is only going through the motions. They have no way of finding out which officer was hoping to make a quick buck. The problem the Prison Service is facing is that Trevor will never reveal his source.

DAY 38

Back to the visitor from Belmarsh. Mr Greenacre tells me to expect a senior security officer to interview me on Tuesday morning, which means that, with luck, I'll miss pottery. I'll brief you fully next Tuesday.

11.00 am

Exercise. My legs are still aching from the gym session, so I find it quite hard to maintain the pace of Jimmy (twenty-nine) and Darren (thirty-five) as they march round the perimeter of the jail, but I'm damned if I'm going to admit it. They are chatting away about an unusual use of mirrors. Every cell has a five-by-five-inch steel mirror screwed to the wall. Jimmy is telling us about two West Indian prisoners who between them raised enough money to purchase a ghetto blaster and a pair of loud speakers. He describes how they went about arranging to listen to the same music in two different cells.

The first prisoner levered his thin steel mirror off the wall and inserted a coil of wire through one of the tiny holes in a corner. Every evening, after the nine o'clock flap check, he would slip the mirror under his door, then in one movement, slide it across the corridor until it reached the door opposite. After a few days, he could perform this skill as proficiently as any basketball player dunking a ball through a hoop.

The second prisoner then took the wire and attached it to his speaker so that both men could listen to the same music emanating from one source. Ingenious but – I'm told by anyone who lived within a mile of the jail – unnecessary, because on a still evening you could have danced to the music in Freiston town hall.

12 noon

Lunch. England are 200 for 3 and putting up a spirited fight. During the lunch interval I visit Sergio in his cell. He wastes no words, immediately informing me that he has spoken to his brother in Bogotá. He always sounds like a man who has only ten units left on his phonecard. Of course, he may turn out to be a con man who has no intention of trying to find a Botero.

In any case nothing can be done until Sergio has completed his sentence. He is due to be deported on 27 September, a month from today, by which time we expect to have worked out a plan to purchase a Botero. Win or lose, I'll keep you briefed.

3.00 pm

I have my hair cut by Matt (arson for insurance, failed to convince Cornhill or the jury, and was sentenced to three years). Matt has the reputation of being the best barber in the prison. In fact several prison officers also have their hair cut by him. In his last prison, while serving time for a previous offence, Matt enrolled on a hair-styling course, so now he's a semi-professional. He has all the proper equipment, and within moments of sitting on a chair in the corridor outside his cell, I'm in no doubt about his skill. I need to look neat and tidy for Friday, when Mary and William hope to visit me again. I haven't forgotten that Mary commented on the length of my hair when she last came to Wayland.

When Matt's finished the job he even produces a second mirror so I can see the back of my head. He's not Daniel Hersheson, but for ten units of a phonecard he's a pretty good imitation.

DAY 38

6.00 pm

At close of play England are 314 for 8 after a gritty 124 not out by Ramprakash assisted by Gough, who was clinging in there helping to avoid another follow on. The two of them enter the pavilion needing another 31 runs to make Australia bat again.

A couple of years ago Darren Gough asked me to conduct the auction at his London testimonial dinner at the Dorchester. As a huge fan of Darren's, I happily agreed. When the event finally materialized it fell in the middle of my trial. Mr Justice Potts made it clear to my silk that I should not honour the agreement, even though my name was already printed in the programme. After all, it might influence the jury into believing that I am a charitable man, and I suspect that was the last thing Mr Justice Potts would have wanted.

I'm feeling pretty low, so decide to use the other ten units left on my card to phone Mary. There's no response. I can't get in touch with William or James as they are both abroad. I sit on the end of my bed and recall the words of La Rochefoucauld: *Absence diminishes mediocre passions and increases great ones, as the wind extinguishes candles and fans fire.*

DAY 39   SUNDAY 26 AUGUST 2001

6.16 am

Sunday is always the longest day in prison. Wayland is short-staffed and there is nothing for inmates to do other than watch wall-to-wall television. In Belmarsh, chapel was a respite as it got you out of your cell, but in Wayland you're out of your cell without anything to keep you occupied. Mind you, I'd much rather be in Wayland than locked up in Belmarsh for twenty-two hours a day. I write for a couple of hours.

8.20 am

Breakfast. While I'm waiting in the queue for the hotplate, I get talking to a West Indian who is on my landing. He asks if he can have my *Times* and *Sunday Times* when I've finished with them. I agree to his request if, in return, he will show me how to clean my cell floor. I only mention this because the West Indians keep the cleanest cells. They are not satisfied with sweeping out the dust and dirt, but spend hours buffing up the linoleum floor until you can see your face in it. Although I shower, shave and put on fresh clothes every day, as well as make my bed and have everything in place before the cell door is opened at 8 am, I never look as smart or have as clean a cell as any of the West Indians on my spur.

DAY 39

9.30 am

On my way to the library I slip in behind a man who frightens me. He has an evil face and is one of those prisoners who is proud to describe himself as a career criminal. He is a burglar by profession, and I'm somewhat surprised to see him heading off towards the library with a pile of glossy, coffee-table books under his arm. I try to make out the titles on the spines while we're on the move: *The Encyclopaedia of Antiques*, *Know Your Antiques* and *Antiques in a Modern Market*.

'Are you interested in antiques?' I ask innocently.

'Yeah, I'm making a careful study of them.'

'Are you hoping to work in the antiques trade when you've completed your sentence?'

'I suppose you could say that,' he replies. 'I'm sick of nicking 'em only to find out they're fuckin' worthless. From now on I'll know what to fuckin' look for, won't I?'

You would think that after five weeks of mixing with criminals, night and day, I couldn't still be taken by surprise. It serves to remind me again of Lisa Dada's words about despising burglars, not to mention my own naivety.

10.00 am

In the library I get talking to an older prisoner called Ron (ABH). Most inmates tell me they never want to return to prison, especially the older ones who have served long sentences. But, time and again, they'll add the rider, 'That doesn't mean I won't, Jeff. Getting a job when you have a criminal record is virtually impossible, so you stay on the dole, until you slip back into a life of crime.'

It's a vicious circle for those who leave prison with their

statutory £90, NFA (no fixed abode) and little prospect of work. I don't know the answer, although I accept there is little you can do for people who are genuinely evil, and not much for those who are congenitally stupid. But the first-offence prisoners who want a second chance often leave prison only to find that for the rest of their lives the work door is slammed in their face.

I accept that perhaps only around 20 per cent of prisoners would be worth special treatment, but I would like to see someone come up with a solution for this particular group, especially the first-time offenders. And how many of you reading this diary can honestly say you've never committed a crime? For example:

(a) Smoked cannabis (5 million), crack cocaine (300,000), heroin (250,000)
(b) Stolen something – anything
(c) Fiddled your expenses
(d) Taken a bus or train and not paid for the ticket
(e) Not declared your full income to the taxman
(f) Been over the alcohol limit when driving
(g) Driven a vehicle without tax or insurance
(h) Brought in something from abroad and not paid import tax

I have recently discovered that those very people who commit such crimes often turn out to be the most sanctimonious hypocrites, including one leading newspaper editor. It's the truly honest people who go on treating one decently, as I've found from the thousands of letters I've received from the general public over the past few weeks.

DAY 39

10.45 am

Chapel. We're back to a congregation of eleven. The service is Holy Communion, and I'm not sure I care for the modern version. I must be getting old, or at least old-fashioned.

The service is conducted by John Framlington, resplendent in a long white robe to go with his white beard and head of white hair. He must be well into his seventies and he looks like a prophet. A local Salvation Army officer preaches the sermon, with the theme that we all make mistakes, but that does not mean that we cannot be saved. Once he has delivered his message, he joins John to dispense the bread and wine to his little flock. During the singing of the last hymn, John walks off down the aisle and disappears. We are all left literally standing, not quite sure what to do next. A female face peeps out from behind the organ, and decides to continue playing. This brave little gesture is rewarded by everyone repeating the last verse. When we've delivered the final line of *'O Blessed Jesu, Save Us'* John comes running back down the aisle. He turns to face his congregation, apologizes, blesses us and then disappears for a second time. He's a good man, and it's generous of him still to be giving his time every Sunday for such a motley crew as us.

11.45 am

When I return to my spur after chapel, I find that it has been 'locked off' and we are unable to get into our cells. A small crowd is gathering at the entrance of the spur, and I am informed by Darren that our cells are being searched for phonecards. It seems that one of the prisoners has shaved off the silver lining on the top of his card (see plate section) as this allows him to have a longer period for each unit. Not a great crime you might consider, remembering that we're in a den of thieves. But what you won't realize is that the next person who makes a phone call will find that BT automatically retrieves those stolen units. Result: the next prisoner will be robbed blind.

The next inmate on the phone that morning turned out to be a voluble West Indian called Carl (GBH) who, when his last ten units were gobbled up in seconds, never stopped effing and blinding all the way to the PO's office. The spur was closed down in seconds, and Carl had unwittingly given the 'prison search team' an excuse to go through everyone's personal belongings.

When the gate to the cells is eventually unlocked, a team of three officers comes out carrying a sackful of swag. My bet is that the offending phonecard is not among their trophies, but several other illicit goods are. I return to my cell to find that nothing of mine has been touched. Even my script lies in exactly the same place as I left it. I take this as a compliment.

12 noon

Lunch. England have progressed to 40 for 1, but the ominously dark clouds that appear over Wayland are also, it seems, unpaid visitors at the Oval. I turn my attention to the Sunday papers. The *Sunday Mirror*, that bastion of accuracy, tells its readers that I defended myself from another inmate with a cricket bat. I gave you a full ball-by-ball summary of that match, and the only thing I tried to threaten – and not very successfully – was the ball. The article then goes on to say that I am paying protection money to a prisoner called Matthew McMahon. There is no inmate at Wayland called Matthew McMahon. They add that payment is made with £5 phonecards. There are no £5 phonecards. The funny thing is that some inmates are shocked by this:

they had assumed the papers reported accurately, and it wasn't until I took up residence that they realized how inaccurate the press can be.

2.00 pm

Exercise. We are allowed out for an hour, rather than forty-five minutes, which is a welcome bonus. As we walk round, I get teased by a lot of prisoners who say they are willing to protect me if I'll give them a £5 phonecard. Some ask how come you have a £5 phonecard when the rest of us only have £2 phonecards. Others add that I can hit them with my cricket bat whenever I want to. I confess that this wouldn't be so amusing if Jimmy and Darren were not accompanying me. Certainly, being the butt of everyone's humour inside, as well as outside, begins to tell on one. Jimmy has also read the story in the *Sunday Mirror* and what worries him is who to believe in the latest row between Ken Clarke and Iain Duncan Smith concerning immigration. I tell Jimmy that only one thing is certain: although the result of the leadership election will not be announced for another two weeks (12 September), 70 per cent of the 318,000 electorate have cast their votes, and I assure him that IDS* is already the next leader of the Tory party.

'Can I risk a bet on that?' asks Darren.

'Yes, if you can find anyone stupid enough to take your wager.'

'The spur bookie is offering 1–3 on Duncan Smith.'

'Those are still good odds, because you can't lose unless he drops down dead.'

---

*I note that he is now referred to as IDS by his supporters. I presume this is a desperate attempt to get over the next Tory leader having a double-barrelled name.

Shaun's alternative cover

JIMMY

Captain of everything

DALE

Big Mac

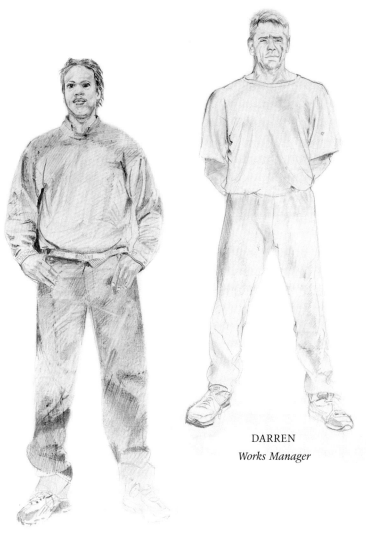

DARREN
Works Manager

NIGEL
Preacher

JULES
Listener

Shaun's montage

Prison-issue £2 phonecard
(note the silver edge)

Typical cell

View from my cell window

THE CARD PLAYERS, 1989 (190 x 240 cm)   BOTERO

Peter Brookes' cartoon 'Nature Notes on Osama Bin Laden
as a poisonous mushroom' (*The Times*, 6 October 2001)

'The bookie or Iain Duncan Smith?' asks Jimmy.

'Either,' I reply.

'Good,' says Darren. 'Then I'll put three Mars bars on Duncan Smith as soon as we get back to the spur.'

4.00 pm

I visit Sergio in his cell to be given a lesson on emeralds. I'll let you know why later. Sergio takes his time telling me that emeralds are to Colombia what diamonds are to South Africa. When he's finished his tutorial, I ask him if it would be possible for his brother to find an emerald of the highest quality. He looks puzzled.

'What sort of price do you have in mind?' he asks.

'Around ten thousand dollars,' I tell him.

He nods. 'I'll see what I can do.' He looks at his watch and adds, 'I'll speak to my brother immediately.'

5.00 pm

Sunday supper is always a bag of crisps and a lemon mousse. However, this evening we are offered two lemon mousses because, I note, the sell-by date on the lid is 25 August.

7.00 pm

At last there's something worth watching on television. *Victoria and Albert* with a cast to kill for. Nigel Hawthorne, Diana Rigg, Peter Ustinov, Jonathan Pryce, David Suchet, John Wood and Richard Briers.

It only serves to remind me how much I miss live theatre, though at times I feel I'm getting enough drama at the Theatre Royal, Wayland.

DAY 40   MONDAY 27 AUGUST 2001

6.08 am

Forty days and forty nights, and, like Our Lord, I feel it's time to come out of the wilderness and get on with some work, despite the fact it's a bank holiday. I write for two hours.

8.15 am

Breakfast. Corn Pops (for a change), UHT milk, a slice of bread and marmalade. I stare at the golly on the jar. I read yesterday in one of the papers that he's no longer politically correct and will be replaced by a character created by Roald Dahl and illustrated by Quentin Blake. I like golly, he's been a friend for years. As a man without an ounce of prejudice in him, I am bound to say I think the world has gone mad.

9.00 am

I call Mary, who is furious with the Home Office. Winston Churchill has written to the Home Secretary, David Blunkett, asking why I'm still in a Category C jail, and Winston has received a reply from Stephen Harrison, David Blunkett's private secretary, suggesting that Lady Archer 'is satisfied that this is the best that can be hoped for'. Home Office officials obviously don't listen to the *Today* programme, or read any newspapers. It doesn't augur well for justice being done to those prisoners who do not have a supportive family. Mary will write to Martin Narey today and put the record straight. My solicitor has not yet received a reply from DCS Perry. Perhaps he's still on holiday. She's also written to the governor of Wayland – also no reply. Thank God I'm not locked up in Russia.

Now I'm no longer on the induction spur, I'm allowed to have my own plate, bowl and mug. Mary promises to dispatch all three today. I can't wait to be rid of the grey plastic set, even if they won't allow me to replace the plastic knife, fork and spoon. Mary tells me that the letters of support are still pouring in, and says she'll send a selection for me to read, plus a list of friends who want to visit me in prison. She confirms that she and William are hoping to visit me on Friday.

9.15 am

A block are playing C block at football, and Jimmy (captain of everything) asks if I'd like to be linesman, knowing it will get me out of my cell for at least an hour. How considerate, I tell him, but I don't know the rules, and I feel sure that there's more to it than just putting your flag in the air when the ball goes out. Fortunately, one of our reserves is fully proficient in the laws of the game, and runs up and down the line behind me, making me look quite competent.

The first player I have to adjudicate offside is Jimmy, who makes no protest and immediately raises his arm. The true character of a person cannot be hidden on a playing field.

By half-time we are two down. However, in the second half,

we pull one back and just before the final whistle, Carl (GBH, phonecard problem) thumps in a blinder from twenty yards to level the score. As he is in the next cell to me, I can expect several graphic replays in the corridor, with the yardage becoming longer by the day.

12.15 pm

Lunch: Toad-in-the-hole (vegetarian sausage) and peas.

3.00 pm

Exercise. We've managed about two circuits when Darren, Jimmy and I are joined by what can only be described as a gang of yobs, whose leader is a stockily built youth of about five foot six, with two rings in his nose and one in each ear. From what I can see of his neck, arms and chest, it doesn't look as if there's anywhere left on his body to needle another tattoo. As soon as he opens his mouth every other word is fucking-this and fuck-ing-that. I'm no longer shocked by this, but I am surprised by the smell of alcohol on his breath. My usual approach when faced with this situation is to answer any question quietly and courteously. I've heard enough stories about prisoners being knifed in the yard over the slightest provocation to do other-wise. But as there are no questions, just abuse hurled at me and my wife, there's not much I can say in reply. Jimmy and Darren close in, not a good sign, but after another circuit, the young thug and his gang of four back off and go and sit against the fence and glare at us.

The Home Office could do worse than invite Darren to sit on one of their committees and advise them on prison policy. He is, after all, far better informed than Stephen Harrison, and therefore the Home Secretary. After a spell in Borstal, and two terms in prison, Darren would be a considerable asset to the drugs debate. He adds that when he was first sent to jail, some fifteen years ago, about 30 per cent of prisoners smoked cannabis and only about 10 per cent were on heroin.

'And today?' I ask.

'Around twenty to thirty per cent are still on cannabis, with approximately the same percentage, if not more, on heroin. And while the present regulations are in place, there's no hope of dealing with the problem. Only last week, a prisoner out on his first town visit returned with five hundred pounds' worth of heroin stuffed up his backside, and every addict in the prison knew about his cache within the hour. They were, if they could afford it, smoking and jabbing themselves all night.'

'But surely the prisoner in question, not to mention his customers, will be caught?'

'The drugs unit interviewed him the following morning. They couldn't prove anything, but it's the last town visit he'll make before he's released – on the grounds of "reasonable suspicion".'

'More fool him,' says Jimmy, who goes out on a town visit once a month. 'Some of them will do anything—' The group of yobs decide to rejoin us, so I have to face another barrage of abuse. I sometimes wish Mr Justice Potts could do just one circuit with me, but it's too late, my case was his last, and he was clearly determined to go out with a bang. When we're called back in, I'm not unhappy to return to the peace and safety of my cell.

DAY 40

4.07 pm

Sergio turns up to tell me the details of a conversation he's had with his brother in Bogotá.

'Tomorrow my brother will travel to the green mountains and select an emerald,' declares Sergio. He will then have it valued and insured. He will also send one gold necklace (18 carat). They sell at a tenth of the price they charge in England. I assure him that, if I decide to buy it, I will make a payment direct to his bank the day after he has been deported. This means he has to put a great deal of trust in me, which he seems happy to do. He accepts that the transaction cannot take place while both of us are still in jail. If he's successful, I'll have more confidence in his claim that he can produce a Botero at a sensible price.

5.00 pm

Darren and I play a couple of games of backgammon, and I'm thankful to have found something I can beat him at. He takes revenge by completing *The Times* crossword before supper.

6.00 pm

Supper: beans on toast and an extra lemon mousse stamped with yesterday's sell-by date.

7.00 pm

I watch the concluding episode of *Victoria and Albert*, every moment of which I thoroughly enjoy.

10.00 pm

Darren lends me his copy of *The Prisons Handbook* – a sort of Relais & Chateaux guide of jails in England and Wales. I accept Mr Meanwell's opinion that once my D-cat has been reinstated, I should apply for Spring Hill in Buckinghamshire, which is the best-located open prison for both London and Cambridge.

DAY 41   TUESDAY 28 AUGUST 2001

6.00 am

I write for two hours.

8.15 am

Breakfast. It's Shredded Wheat again. Eat one, save one.

9.00 am

Pottery. I take my new book, *Arts and Artists*, along to my class to while away the two-hour period. It doesn't seem to bother anyone that I'm not working on a sculpture as long as I'm studying some medium of art.

Shaun appears to be depressed, which could be nothing more than the melancholy of an artist lost in his thoughts. After an hour of painting, he opens his sketch book to reveal an excellent drawing of a Wayland landscape (fairly bleak) and another of a prison door. Then he confides why he is so low. Probation have decided not to let him out two months early on a tag because he failed to appear in court.* However, this two-

---

* The Probation Service can refuse tagging on the following grounds: a) reoffending whilst previously on bail; b) failing to appear in court; c) providing an unsatisfactory address.

month hold-up will pose some problems for both of us. The quality of the paper, pencils, pastels and oils that are available at Wayland are obviously not up to professional standards, so it may become necessary to enlist the help of a member of the art department to purchase the materials he needs. Shaun will have to select someone who believes in his talent, and more importantly, he needs to trust me enough to believe I will pay him back after he's been released in November. A member of staff tells me later that Shaun is the most talented prisoner they have come across since they started working in prisons. Our conversation is interrupted by a security officer who says I'm wanted in reception.

10.12 am

A senior officer from Belmarsh is waiting for me in the room with the comfortable chairs. The governor of Belmarsh has put her in charge of the investigation into the theft of seven pages of my diary. You will recall that Trevor Kavanagh, the *Sun's* political editor, handed the script over to Mary, who in turn passed the seven handwritten pages on to my lawyer.

The officer tells me that she has been in the Prison Service for nearly twenty years, and adds that she isn't on a whitewash expedition. She makes it clear from the outset that the seven pages of script could not have been stolen by a prisoner, as they wouldn't have had access to a photocopier. She goes even further and admits that they have narrowed the likely culprit down to one of two officers.

She then hands me a photocopy of my first seven pages, and after reading only a few lines I recall how distraught I was at Belmarsh. I confirm that I had written these pages when I was in the medical centre on my first day, but I have no way of knowing when they were removed or returned, or by whom. I only recall leaving the cell once in the first twenty-four hours, and that was for a forty-five-minute break in the exercise yard. She nods, as if she not only knows when I left my cell, but exactly how many minutes I was out of the room.

'You were then escorted across to B block to begin your induction. Did you have the script with you at the time?'

'Yes, I posted the pages to my PA every three or four days, but not before they were checked by Roy the censor, who I didn't meet until the third day, so it can't have been him.'

'No, it certainly wasn't Roy,' she replied, 'because the *Sun* received the material the following morning. And in any case, Roy's bright enough to understand the law of copyright. Whoever did this must have been surprised and disappointed that the *Sun* wouldn't touch it.'

She leaves after about an hour, promising to let me know the outcome of her investigation.*

12.15 pm

Lunch: vegetable soup and a chocolate wafer. Sergio slips me a banana.

2.00 pm

In order to make up my five lessons a week, I have to attend an education class on a Tuesday afternoon.

The Education Department is situated next to the library, and once I've signed in, I report to room one as instructed. I

---

* No member of the prison staff has ever reported back to me or my lawyers on the outcome of this enquiry.

enter a classroom containing twenty small desks set out in a U-shape facing a teacher. Her name is Ms Jocelyn Rimmington, and she looks as if she's been plucked straight out of an Evelyn Waugh novel. Her job is a difficult one, and I watch her carry it out with consummate skill and ingenuity. She has eight charges, including me. The prisoner she's talking to is learning basic English so he can take a plumbing exam. The inmate on his right is reading Chaucer as part of an A level course, and on his left is an inmate who is learning to read and write. The remaining four prisoners are preparing for GCSE English. Ms Rimmington moves slowly and methodically from desk to desk, answering each and every question thrown at her until she reaches me.

'Wendy tells me that you're in the middle of writing another book.'

'Yes, I am,' I reply.

'And she thinks the best thing would be for you to carry on with it, until we decide what to do with you.'

I don't demur; after all, what's the point of telling this charming lady that I would prefer to do something more productive. It's obvious that either Wendy Sergeant, who is head of the department, or those above her, lack the imagination of the education department at Belmarsh, who had me conducting a creative writing class before the end of my first week.

5.00 pm

Supper. I eat very little because the only gym session I can attend today is at six o'clock.

DAY 41

6.00 pm

Gym. Complete a full session, mainly because half the regulars are out playing football. Today is the final trial before they select the team for the first match on Sunday. As I cannot be present at Lord's for the one day final between Somerset and Leicestershire, I'll have to settle for Wayland versus RAF Methwold.

7.30 pm

After a long press, press, press-button shower, I return to the cell and dry myself with a mean little rough green towel. Sergio knocks on the door, walks in, plonks himself on the end of the bed and without any preamble, starts to give me another lecture on emeralds.

'Seventy per cent of the world's emeralds come from Colombia,' he proclaims. 'Over twenty thousand stones change hands in Bogotá every day. The emerald is second only in popularity and value to the diamond, and its size is measured in the same way (carat). The very finest stones,' he continues, 'are known as "drops of oil" because if you stare into the centre of the stone, you can see what appears to be just that. We must make sure that ours is at least four carats, and that the drop of oil is there for all to see.

'For one stone, the price can range according to quality,' continues Sergio, 'from a few hundred dollars to several millions.' He anticipates the stone his brother selects could be on its way to London as early as next week. Because Sergio went to the same school as the niece of the owner of 'the mountain', he hopes his brother will be able to deal direct, cutting out any middlemen. As his brother doesn't know that Sergio is ensconced in an English jail, I wonder why he isn't puzzled by the fact that he can't call back. I don't ask.

8.00 pm

Pottery followed by an interview with the lady from Belmarsh, followed by education, followed by the gym, followed by Sergio and his lecture on emeralds, interspersed with three writing sessions. I'm exhausted.

I fall asleep fully dressed during the *Ten O'Clock News*. When I wake, it's just after eleven. I undress, use the loo, climb into my tiny bed, and fall asleep a second time.

DAY 42   WEDNESDAY 29 AUGUST 2001

5.19 am

I have now undergone the same three-week induction cycle at HMP Wayland as I did at Belmarsh. My routine, compared with my life outside, is far more regimented, conforming to a daily pattern, and then a weekly one. So I have decided, as from today, to comment only on highlights, rather than simply repeat the numbing routine with which you must now be familiar.

6.00 am

I write for two hours and then eat the other Shredded Wheat covered in milk supplied by Sergio.

9.00 am

Paul, one of the tutors, brings in a set of slides to the art class, and gives us a lecture on the Impressionists. I am stunned that Shaun, such a talented artist, has never heard of Pissarro or Sisley. He also admits that he has visited a gallery only two or three times in his life. The slide show is so popular with the other prisoners that Paul promises to bring in examples of other artists next week when he will introduce us to Magritte, Rothko and Warhol, amongst others.

12 noon

After lunch, I go to the gym. When I've finished my programme, I jump on the scales to discover that I'm still losing weight – nearly a stone since I've been in prison. Just as I'm leaving, the football coach calls me into his office and asks if I would attend the first fixture of the season on Sunday, and write a match report for the prison magazine. I readily agree, only relieved he didn't invite me to play.

4.00 pm

Sergio joins me in my cell to tell me the latest on the emerald hunt before continuing with his tutorial. The majority of emeralds mined in Colombia come from one mountain that has been owned by the same family for generations. Most of the stones that come out of Colombia are exported to Japan, but Sergio is hoping, when he returns to Bogotá, to start diverting some of these gems to Europe. He is becoming more ambitious every day.

He also informs me that trading in emeralds is every bit as dangerous as dealing in drugs. Every day eight helicopters fly back and forth from the mountain to Bogotá airport with four armed guards on each and another twenty private police waiting for them on the runway. On the mountain there are 300 workers and 100 armed guards. A peasant (his description) can earn as much as $50,000 a year if, and he repeats if, he is lucky enough to dig up any high-quality gems.

'But what about theft?' I ask. 'How do they deal with that?'

'One or two of the workers are stupid enough to consider stealing the odd stone, but they quickly discover that there is no judge or jury on the mountain.'

'So how do they dispense justice?'

'Instantly,' he replies. 'One of the guards shoots the culprit in front of the other workers, who then bury him.'

'But you could swallow a stone, and then sell it in Bogotá, where you've already told me that twenty thousand emeralds change hands in the marketplace every day.'

'True,' Sergio replies. 'But you will still be caught, because the family has over a hundred spotters in the market, night and day. If a dealer ever traded with a thief, they would immediately be cut off from their source of supply. And in time the thief will have to return to the mountain if he hopes to go on trading. In any case, the workers know they will have a far higher standard of living than their fellow countrymen as long as they remain employed on the mountain.'

'But they could take the gems abroad and make a fortune?'

'Most peasants,' says Sergio, 'have never travelled further than the next village, and none of them speaks anything but mountain Spanish, which even I can't understand. Even the owner of the mountain can still only converse in his native tongue and would never consider leaving Colombia. It is only because of my four years in an English jail,' continues Sergio, 'that it's now possible for me to act as a go-between and consider the export business. And you now also have an advantage, Jeffrey, because your rivals cannot easily buy or sell paintings from Colombia.' I raise an eyebrow. 'I am being deported in four weeks' time, and can never return to Britain unless I am willing to risk completing the remaining four years of my sentence.'

'An enterprising dealer could always fly to Bogotá.'

'Not wise,' says Sergio. 'Fair-haired, blue-eyed people are not welcome in Bogotá, and especially not on the mountain.' He goes on to explain: 'It would be assumed that you are an American, and your chances of making it back to the airport would be about as good as a peasant caught stealing.' No wonder it's a closed market.

My tutorial comes to an end when an officer bellows, 'Lock up.' I run out of Sergio's cell to return to the real world, because I need the five minutes to join the queue and change my sheets, pillowcase, towels and gym kit. Don't forget it's Wednesday, and if you don't get to the laundry room before they close, you have to wait another week.

8.00 pm

When I get back to my cell I find a biography of *Oscar Wilde* by Sheridan Morley awaiting me on my bed. I had asked Steve (conspiracy to murder, chief librarian) to reserve this book for me. Nothing like a personal delivery service.

I become so engrossed in Wilde's life that I miss the *Ten O'Clock News.* I have reached Oscar's first trial by the time I put the book down. I must save the second trial for tomorrow night.

Not a bad day, but please don't think, even for one moment, that it's therefore been a good one.

DAY 43   THURSDAY 30 AUGUST 2001

8.45 am

I arrive for my pottery class to find it's been cancelled because the teacher hasn't turned up. Shaun tells me this is a regular occurrence, and he seems to be the only person who is disappointed because he was hoping to finish a painting. It gives me another couple of hours to write, while the other prisoners are happy to go off to the gym or their cells while still being paid £1.40.

10.45 am

I hear a cry of 'Library' bellowed down the corridor and, as I've just come to the end of another chapter of *Oscar Wilde*, decide to take a break and return *Arts and Artists*. I now know my way around the library and go straight to the art shelves. I select a book entitled *Legendary Gems* by Eric Bruton and add a novel by Robert Goddard.

When I return to my cell I find my laundry is waiting in a neat pile, washed and dried. I look up to see Darren standing on my chair, clipping up a new curtain rail.

'Let me warn you,' he says as he climbs back down off the chair, 'you can't hang yourself from a prison curtain rail.'

'I hadn't given the idea much thought, but why not?' I ask, opening my notebook.

'Because it just clips on, so if you attached a noose to the rail and then jumped off the chair, you'd land on the floor wrapped up in your curtain.'

'So how can I hang myself?' I demand.

'You should have done it at your remand prison,' Darren replies.

'I'm not sure I understand.'

'Most remand prisons are of a Victorian vintage, and have high-level barred windows making the job that much easier.'

'But I was only there for a few days.'

'There are more hangings in the first few days in jail than at any other time.'

'Why?'

'Often the psychological impact of entering prison for the first time causes deep depression, and that's when a prisoner sees suicide as the only way out.'

'So it's less common once you've been transferred?'

'Yes, but I knew a prisoner who still found an original way to kill himself.' I continue to scribble away. 'He was in a cell with a one-up and one-down, and when his room-mate went to work and he was left alone for the rest of the morning he stood the bed up on its end, so that the rail was about seven feet from the ground. He used his belt as a noose, and attached it to the top railing. He then climbed on top, placed his hands in the back of his jeans, rolled off the bed and hanged himself. On the table they found a letter from his girlfriend saying she couldn't wait for three years. If you want to kill yourself, you can always find a way,' Darren adds matter of factly. 'Each year the Prison Service publishes statistics on how many inmates commit suicide. There were ninety-two in 2001,' says Darren, just before he leaves to continue his rounds. 'However, what they don't tell you is how many people die, or commit suicide within six months of being released.' I slowly unpack my washing and stack it on the narrow shelves while I consider what Darren has just told me.

2.00 pm

After lunch I pick up *Legendary Gems* and turn to the chapter on emeralds. Everything Sergio has told me during the past ten days is verified by the author, which gives me more confidence in Sergio. However, two crucial questions remain: does Sergio have the right contacts and can he replace the middlemen? I am pleased to see that Laurence Graff warrants three mentions in the diamond chapter.

To date I haven't mentioned Laurence Graff (of Graff's of Bond Street, Madison Avenue and Monte Carlo), but I'm rather hoping he will agree to value the gem for me. Laurence and I first met at a charity function many years ago when I was the auctioneer. Since then he and his wife, Anne-Marie, have told me many stories about the diamond trade which have found their way into my books. It was Laurence who gave me the idea for the short story 'Cheap at Half the Price'.

3.00 pm

Jimmy rushes into my cell with a large grin on his face. He scowls at Darren's new curtain rail, immediately aware of who must have supplied it.

'I am the bearer of glad tidings,' he says. 'A prisoner on our spur will be leaving tomorrow morning, a week earlier than originally planned. He keeps the cleanest cell on the block. He's even decorated it, and best news of all, it's on the quiet side of the spur, so you'd better have a word with Meanwell before someone else grabs it.'

I'm just about to go off in search of Mr Meanwell, when Jimmy adds, 'He's off today, but he's back on tomorrow morning at 7.30, and don't forget you've got the special needs group at 8.45, so you'd better see him straight after breakfast.' Darren walks in, livid to find Jimmy sitting on the end of my bed. He's obviously picked up the same piece of information and had hoped to be the first to impart it.

'I think you'll find my information was as welcome as your curtain rail,' suggests Jimmy smugly.

'Only if his lordship ends up getting David's cell,' says Darren, well aware that I am playing them against each other. Still, like two children, they find the challenge irresistible.

7.00 pm

After supper, Sergio reveals good news. Having visited the mountain, his brother has selected a 4-carat emerald at a cost of $10,000.

'If my contact confirms that its shop value is twenty thousand, then I'll buy it,' I tell him. 'If not . . .' Sergio looks up and frowns. 'Purchase the emerald,' I continue, 'and have it sent to London. I'll need proper certification, but if my valuer says he can sell me a stone of the same quality at the same price or cheaper, it will all have been a waste of your time, and I'll return the stone to Colombia at my expense.'

'My whole reputation rests on this one stone?' Sergio asks.

'You've got it,' I tell him.

DAY 44   FRIDAY 31 AUGUST 2001

8.21 am

Breakfast. I eat my cereal out of a china bowl, my toast on a plate and drink my milk from a mug. Mary has selected the plate and bowl from the Bridgewater collection and the beaker – a garish object covered in the American stars and stripes – was a gift Will brought back from the States.

When I've finished my breakfast I fill my washbasin with hot water and Fairy Liquid, allowing my newly acquired treasures to soak while I go off in search of Mr Meanwell. The block's senior officer has been off for two days, so was unaware that David had been released six days early,* and that his cell on the enhanced wing has suddenly become available. He'll let me know what he's decided later today.

I return to my cell and find a gathering of West Indians in the corridor. They've come to say farewell to a prisoner who is leaving this morning, having served six years of a nine-year sentence for armed robbery – his first offence.

Most of you reading this will have already formed a picture

---

* This is often a result of police custody days being deducted from the prisoner's sentence.

of him in your mind, as I would have done only a couple of months ago. A young black thug who's better off locked up, and who will probably beat up some other innocent person the moment he's released and be back in prison within a year.

In fact, he is thirty-two years old, five foot eight, slim and good-looking. He was the one who politely asked if he could read my newspapers every evening. And he has used his six years productively. First to pass his GCSEs (five) and two years later A levels in English and History.

No sooner has he departed than Jules appears in the corridor carrying a plastic bag full of his worldly goods. He is taking over Steve's cell. He tells me that the past week has not been a happy one because he's had to share our old cell with a heroin addict who was injecting himself two, sometimes three times a day.

8.45 am

On Friday mornings the gym is taken over by the special needs group. They're an enthusiastic bunch who, despite their problems, bring a range of skills and boundless energy to everything they do. Les performs well on the rowing machine (1,000m in ten minutes), while Robbie enjoys lifting weights and Paul prefers to run. But when it comes to the game of catchball that we always play at the end of any session, Robbie can catch anything that comes his way. He could, and would, happily field in the slips for England.

All of them are chatterboxes, and demand answers to their endless questions. Do you have a father? Do you have a mother? Do you have any brothers or sisters? Are you married? Do you have any children? By the end of the hour's session, I am physically and mentally exhausted, and full of admiration for their carer, Ann, who spends every waking moment with them.

At the end of the session, I watch them leave, chatting, laughing and – I hope – happier. There, but for the grace of God . . .

2.54 pm

Mr Nutbourne opens the cell door. 'You're moving again, Jeffrey,' he says. 'You've been allocated David's old cell on the enhanced spur.' He winks.

'Thank you,' I reply, and prepare for my ninth move in six weeks. The whole process takes less than an hour, because on this occasion I'm assisted by a local removal company: *Darren, Sergio and Jimmy Ltd.*

My new cell is on the ground floor with the enhanced prisoners. Number seventeen is opposite Darren's cell, who has Steve (conspiracy to murder and librarian) on one side, and Jimmy (Ecstasy courier, captain of everything) on the other. The officers describe it as the grown-up spur, and personally select who will be allowed to reside there. To have made it in three weeks is considered quite an achievement, although Darren managed it in four days.

The cells are exactly the same size as in any other part of the prison, but the table on which I'm now working is far larger (four feet by two). I also have an extra cupboard for my possessions, which seem to grow as each day passes, not unlike when you're on holiday.

5.00 pm

Once I've completed my move, I join Darren and Sergio for a walk in the exercise yard. I stop halfway round to watch Shaun sketching Dale. He is still proving to be a restless model, but despite this Shaun is producing a good likeness of him.

6.00 pm

After supper I call Mary (my new spur has a phone of its own, which any self-respecting estate agent would describe as 'an added amenity'). She's full of news, some good, some not so good. The police confirm that they will not be presenting their report on the Simple Truth until they've read the findings of the KPMG report. This won't be handed in to the Red Cross for at least another two, perhaps three weeks. Mary tells me that the police reply to Tony Morton-Hooper's letter was not unhelpful, and she hopes that once the KPMG report is finished, it will only be a matter of days before they move me to an open prison.

I use the remainder of my twenty units catching up with all things domestic, particularly what is happening at the Old Vicarage. When the phonecard flicks out, indicating I have only thirty seconds left, I promise to call again on Sunday. Don't forget, I no longer have an endless source of cards.

As soon as I replace the receiver, Sergio takes over the phone. He has the advantage of being able to hold a conversation in a language no one else on the spur can eavesdrop on, but the disadvantage of needing at least five phonecards every time he dials home.

DAY 44

6.50 pm

When Sergio has finished his call, he joins me in my cell. Now that we're on the same spur, it's no longer necessary for me to try and pretend I'm learning Spanish – he's just another prisoner from across the corridor.

Sergio's brother has selected four emeralds for consideration. He confirms they range in price from ten to fifteen thousand dollars. Once he has made the final choice, I will await a valuation from my expert. His brother claims that any one of the gems would retail on the London market at around $20,000. If this proves to be accurate, then I'll be happy to purchase the selected gem and give it to Mary as her Christmas present. Ah, you've finally discovered why I'm going to all this trouble.

8.15 pm

To my delight, I discover that our spur is unlocked first and banged up last, giving us an extra few minutes at each end of the day. What I enjoy most about being below stairs is the silence, or near silence, compared with the floor above. No rap music, no window warriors and no conversations shouted from one end of the corridor to the other. There is actually a feeling of community on this spur.

I don't bother to turn on the TV this evening as I am totally engrossed in Robert Goddard's *Caught in the Light*. I fall asleep fully dressed. It's been an exhausting day.

DAY 45 SATURDAY 1 SEPTEMBER 2001

8.15 am

The first day of a new month. After breakfast, I arrange with Locke (GBH), the spur painter, to have my new cell redecorated in his spare time. As the tariff has to be agreed in tobacco, and as I have no idea of the going rate, Darren (marijuana only) has agreed to act as my works manager for the transaction.

Once Locke has inspected my cell, he announces it will first need an undercoat of white, which will take him two, two-hour sessions. Darren agrees the price on a daily basis. Tomorrow he will add a coat of cream, and on Monday the cell door, the window ledge and frame plus the square around the wash basin will be painted beige. As far as I can work out, the painter will receive one pound's worth of Golden Virginia (his choice) a day. So the whole job will cost me £3 – which, Darren assures me, is the going rate. The paint, however, will be supplied by Her Majesty's tax payers. Please note that it was Margaret Thatcher who taught me never to say government; 'Governments don't pay taxes, Jeffrey, only tax payers do.'

Locke asks me to vacate my cell while the undercoat is being rolled on because once my bed, table and small cupboard have been pulled away from the walls and left in the centre of the room, there will only be enough space for one person.

I cross the corridor to join Sergio in his cell, where we hold a board meeting. Overnight, Sergio has typed out sixteen questions which he needs answered before he speaks to his brother again. For example: do I want to pay the full insurance cost? – Yes. Do I want the gold necklace to be 9, 14 or 18 carat? – 18 carat. Will I have to pay import tax when the chain and emerald land in London? – Don't know, but I'll find out.

Once Sergio has asked all his questions and written out the answers neatly in Spanish, we move onto item number two on the agenda.

I've received a letter from Chris Beetles, who has carried out considerable research into which South American artists have a worldwide market. He reports that Christie's and Sotheby's have two Latin American sales a year, both held in New York. With the exception of Botero, who has recently passed $2 million for an oil, only Lamand Tamayo regularly fetches $100,000 or more under the hammer. Sergio reads the letter slowly and places it in his file.

11.00 am

Exercise. It's Darren's turn to be sketched by Shaun, and he's proving a bit of a prima donna. He's a very private man who doesn't keep any photographs of himself. He's still grumbling about his participation as we walk out into the yard. We are greeted by Shaun, who is holding a large art pad in his right hand, and a couple of pencils in his left.

Darren reluctantly agrees to pose, but only on two conditions. That the drawing is carried out on the far side of the yard, where few inmates will see him during their perambulations. He also insists that if he doesn't like the result, he will be left out of the final montage. I don't have a lot of choice, so I agree. I can only hope that Shaun will make such a good job of the preliminary sketch that Darren will be converted to the whole idea.

Jimmy and I go off for a circuit while Shaun begins his task. While we stroll round the perimeter, the talk among the inmates is only of football. England are playing Germany tonight, and Wayland are playing Methwold tomorrow. Some of the prisoners lying on the grass against the fence wish Jimmy, our captain, good luck, while another suggests that he couldn't score in a brothel.

By the end of the third circuit, a likeness is appearing on Shaun's sketch pad, but I have no way of knowing how Darren will react. He can be so perverse at times.

By the time we've completed two more circuits, the officers in the yard are beginning to herd us back to our blocks. We stop to look at Shaun's effort. Darren joins us to see the outline image for the first time. It's good, and he knows it. He nods his grudging approval, but finally gives the game away when, as we stroll back into A block, he asks, 'If that's only a sketch before Shaun does the final portrait, can I have it for my mother?' (See plate section.)

12 noon

Standing in the lunch queue I discover from Dumsday (who, Jimmy told me a few days earlier, had adopted an injured crow) that his crow died early this morning, despite his sitting up all night trying to feed it a boiled egg. I return to my cell and eat lunch standing in the middle of the room with the smell of fresh paint all around me. I survey my £3 investment. Locke has made a good start.

DAY 45

2.00 pm

The spur is getting worked up about the match this evening between England and Germany, which is a World Cup qualifying game. I am invited to pull the name of an England player out of a plastic cup, and should my selection score the first goal, I'll win nine Mars bars. I draw Gerard who, Jimmy assures me, has a good chance of scoring. I read in this morning's *Times* that England haven't won a match on German soil since 1965. But I don't pass on this information to a football-mad spur. I glance out of my window to see five rabbits eating the left-over food the prisoners have thrown out of their cell. As we are hemmed in behind a twenty-foot fine-meshed wire fence, I wonder how the rabbits get into the prison. I'll make enquiries.

6.00 pm

On a Saturday, we're banged up after supper but, as I've mentioned, the enhanced spur goes last so we can roam the corridors until six thirty – an extra thirty minutes. I check my TV listings in *The Times* to find that the football is on BBC 1, but clashes with Jane Austen's *Persuasion* on BBC 2. I elect to watch *Persuasion* while the rest of the spur settles down to follow the match. I'm confident that, if England score, the whole prison will let me know.

Just as Miss Elliot meets Captain Wentworth for the first time, the spur erupts with cheering and shouting. I quickly switch channels and watch a replay of Michael Owen scoring for England, which means I've lost a Mars bar. I switch back and continue my vigil with Miss Elliot who, because of her father's financial problems, has had to move from the family's magnificent country home to a smaller residence in Bath. I become

180

deeply engrossed in the drama of lost love when there is another eruption of cheering. I switch over to find England have scored a second goal on the stroke of half-time. I discover that the score is 2–1 in England's favour, so I must have missed the German goal. It was obviously greeted by my fellow inmates in total silence.

I turn back to *Persuasion* to find that Captain Wentworth is flirting (the occasional glance) with our heroine, the one we want him to marry. There is another roar. I can't believe it, and switch across to find our other hero, Michael Owen, has scored again, and England are now leading three goals to one. No sooner have I switched back than there is a further roar, so I return to watch a replay of Owen completing his hat-trick, giving England an unbelievable 4–1 lead.

I flick over to Jane Austen and discover that the handsome Captain Wentworth could be about to marry the wrong girl, but then – an explosion – can it be true? I return to BBC 1 to find Heskey has scored for England and we now lead five goals to one with ten minutes to go. Quickly back to *Persuasion* where our hero and long-suffering heroine have become engaged. No suggestion of sex, not even a kiss. Long live Jane Austen.

10.00 pm

I finish the Robert Goddard book and then climb into my bed which is still in the middle of the room. I fall asleep to the smell of fresh paint and the sound of my fellow inmates reliving every one of those five England goals.

DAY 46   SUNDAY 2 SEPTEMBER 2001

10.00 am

After writing for a couple of hours and having breakfast, I report to the gym in my new capacity as football correspondent for the *Prison News*.

The Wayland team meet in the changing room where they are handed their kit: a light blue shirt, dark blue shorts, blue socks, shin pads and a pair of football boots. As with the cricket match last week, the team are far better equipped than most amateur club sides, and once again all at the tax payers' expense. All four blocks also have their own strip (A block's is yellow and black). I assume this is normal practice for every prison across the country.

Once the team has changed, and very smart they look, we're joined by our coach, Gary, who delivers an unusual team talk. Because the players have been selected from four different blocks and prisoners come and go every week, some of them haven't even met before. The first thing the eleven men and three subs have to do is to announce their names and the positions they'll be playing in. You may well consider that this is an insuperable barrier for any team, but not so, because the opposition also have several disadvantages to contend with. To

182

start with, all of Wayland's fixtures are played at home – think about it – and the rival team are not allowed to bring along any supporters, especially not girlfriends. And when it comes to gamesmanship, our team are in a class of their own, and the officers are just as bad.

The opposition side are met at the gates by sniffer dogs before being searched. The players are then escorted to the changing rooms, accompanied by the boos of prisoners from all four blocks. And if that isn't enough to contend with, they then have to deal with our captain, Jimmy.

Now Jimmy is all charm and bonhomie as he accompanies the opposition side from the changing room onto the pitch. But he does consider it nothing less than his duty to inform the visitors that they should keep a wary eye on Preston, Wayland's main striker.

'Why?' asks the opposing team captain innocently.

'He's in for a double murder – chopped his parents' heads off while they were asleep.' Jimmy pauses. 'Even we don't like him. He's already got a twenty-five-year sentence, and as he's only done three, the occasional broken leg doesn't seem to worry him too much, especially as he's only likely to get a yellow card.'

The truth is that our main striker is in for breaking and entering (rather appropriate) but by the time Jimmy has reached the pitch, the Methwold team is convinced that if Hannibal Lecter were at Wayland he would be relegated to the subs bench.

The first half is a shambles; the ball goes up and down the pitch with little speed and even less purpose. Wayland are trying to get to know each other, while Methwold still aren't sure if they dare risk the occasional tackle. It's 0–0 when the whistle blows for half-time, and frankly no one deserved to score.

The second half is a complete contrast as I'm made aware of the other advantage Wayland has: fitness. All of our team spend at least an hour every day in the gym, rather than at the local pub, and it begins to show. The first goal is headed in by Carl (GBH), after an excellent cross by our 'double-murderer'. The second is scored by Dan (armed robbery), another of our strikers, and the third is added by Hitch (arson). We end up winning 3–0, which augurs well for the rest of the season. Perhaps we could even win the league cup this year. But it's back to disadvantages, because three of the team, including Jimmy, are due to be released before Christmas, and the side we will field at the end of the season will bear no resemblance to the one that lined up for the opening encounter.

Despite the team's glorious victory, some of the officers are irritated by the fact that they've been made to hang around until we return for a late lunch. With the exception of Mr Nutbourne, who makes sure that the team is fed, they can't wait to get us banged up and go off duty.

The relationship between officers and prisoners is always conducted on a tightrope which both sides walk every day. The officers on duty that Sunday morning unwisely miss an opportunity to make their own lives easier. A few words of praise and allowing an extra minute or two in the shower would have paid huge dividends in the long run. Instead, the victors return to their cells with shrivelled-up pieces of meat covered in cold gravy, unable to shower until we are unlocked again in two hours' time. Of course I understand that the prison is not run for the convenience of the prisoners, but here was an opportunity for the officers to make their own life easier in the long term. They botched it, with the exception of Mr Nutbourne, who will get far more cooperation and respect from the inmates in the future.

2.00 pm

Board meeting. Sergio has talked to his brother in Bogotá. The four emeralds that his brother initially selected have been short-listed to two and, along with a member of the family who owns the mountain, Sergio's brother will make the final selection tomorrow. He has also assured him that, whichever one they choose, the gem would retail at three times the price in a London shop. As for paintings, Sergio's school friend has told him that, through Sergio's mother, she has made an appointment with Botero's mother, and will report back by the end of the week. My heart leaps at the thought of finally owning a Botero.

4.00 pm

While I do a circuit with Jimmy, Shaun continues to draw Darren, who surprisingly now proves, unlike Dale, to be a still and patient model. I'm delighted with the preliminary sketches and, more importantly, so is Darren. While Shaun is sketching, I ask Darren about the rabbits. The rabbits, it seems, are no fools. They know when the prisoners are fed, and burrow under the fence to gather up the food thrown out of the windows by the inmates after lock-up. They are occasionally joined by a family of ducks. But, and there is always a but in prison, there is also a fox lurking around, who is even more cunning. He also enters under the fence after lock up, and catches the rabbits while they nibble the food dropped from the prisoners' table. The fox has also worked out that there is no such thing as 'The Wayland Hunt'.

I tell Shaun that I've spoken to Chris Beetles and hope that it will result in his being in receipt (I select the words carefully) of the highest quality drawing paper, chalks, watercolours and pencils, so that his final effort can't be blamed on his tools. He's delighted.

DAY 46

6.00 pm

Early lock up because of staff shortages. I will have to remain in my five paces by three cell for the next fourteen hours.

I start reading Jeeves. What a different world Bertie Wooster lived in. How would Bertie have coped with Wayland? I suppose Jeeves would have volunteered to take his place.*

---

* P. G. Wodehouse spent some time in a German jail during the Second World War. He was later accused of 'collaborating with the Germans' by the British press and then spent the rest of his life in America, which he considered exile.

DAY 47   MONDAY 3 SEPTEMBER 2001

5.43 am

I wake to the smell of fresh paint, so I feel I should bring you up to date on my redecoration programme. The white undercoat was finished yesterday, and while I was at pottery Locke (GBH, spur painter) added a coat of magnolia to the walls and beige to the door, window ledge and skirting board.

I have always liked brick as a medium, but I find the solid block of white a little unimaginative, so during pottery class this morning I'm going to suggest to Shaun that he might design a pattern for the walls, and then find out if Locke is willing to add 'interior decorator' to his portfolio. It may well cost me another couple of pounds, but I could then enter my cell for the Turner Prize.

9.00 am

During pottery class, Shaun begins to knock out a few ideas for a pattern on my walls, and very imaginative they are.

He then produces his sketch pad and shows me his latest ideas for the book cover. The first one is a cell door with eyes peeping through the little flap, while the second is a prisoner's card as displayed outside every cell. I wonder if he could somehow combine the two.*

12 noon

After lunch I make notes in preparation for a visit from William, James and David, my driver of fifteen years. Once I've done this I have to learn each of the headings by heart, as I'm not allowed to take anything into the visitors' room. I count how many topics need to be covered – William eight, James nine, David five. After that I'll have to rely on my memory.

1.30 pm

I shower and shave before putting on a new pair of jeans and a freshly ironed, blue-striped shirt. I have never been vain, but I am far too proud to allow the boys to see me looking unkempt – and wondering if prison has got the better of me.

2.00 pm

As I leave the cell to join my children, Locke strolls in. I haven't yet summoned up the courage to tell him about my idea for further redecoration, and I suspect I'll end up leaving the negotiations to my works manager, Darren.

When I arrive in the visitors' area, I am searched for the first time in over a week, but compared to Belmarsh this exercise is fairly cursory. I don't know if suspected drug addicts and dealers receive different treatment. I'm once again allocated table four–

---

* The cell card was eventually used on the back of *Volume One – Belmarsh: Hell*.

teen, where I take my place in the red chair, leaving the three blue chairs vacant. I look around the room that holds about seventy tables, but only five are occupied by prisoners. This is because of the breakdown of the prison computer, which has thrown the visiting schedule into chaos.

James is the first through the door, surprise, surprise, followed by William, then David. Once we have completed the hugs and greetings I explain that I wish to allocate the two hours judiciously. The first half hour I'll spend with William, the second with James and the third with David, before having the final half hour with all three of them.

While the other two disappear, Will updates me on the KPMG report and my D-cat reinstatement. Mary has been in touch with Gillian Shephard, currently my local MP, who has promised to contact the governor of Wayland and make it clear that once the police have dropped their enquiry, I ought to be moved on to an open prison as quickly as possible. Mind you, the Prison Service's idea of as quickly as possible . . .

Will also reports that he hopes to return to America in about three weeks as he has been offered several new commissions for documentaries. To his surprise, he's also been approached about some work in London.

While I try to recall my eight points, Will briefs me about his mother. Mary is holding up well in the circumstances, but he feels that she has probably been most affected by the whole experience.

I then ask if Will could do three things for me. First, give Chris Beetles £200 in order that Shaun will be in receipt of the art materials he needs. Second, select a bowl and plate from the Bridgewater collection and send them to Darren at Wayland, a man whose kindness I will never be able to repay properly. Finally, I ask if he will somehow get hold of my special Staedtler liquid pens, because— Will points to the tray in front of me, where I see he has slipped two behind a can of Diet Coke. I smile, but wonder if I can get the treasure back to my cell without it being confiscated.

Once I've completed my list, he brings me up to date on his social life. Ten minutes later he leaves me and James takes his place.

I spend some considerable time briefing James on Sergio's background, and explain how three weeks in prison, in such intense circumstances, is the equivalent of about three months on the outside. He nods, as he's well aware that this is only background before I broach the real subject. Having established Sergio's credentials, about which I tell him I have only my instinct to go on, we then discuss the subject of emeralds in great detail. I explain for an investment of $10,000, subject to valuation, we will acquire one emerald which will arrive in London later this week. If Sergio turns out to have been honest about the emerald, it might then be worth getting him to search for a Botero.

'If he doesn't manage to find any paintings,' I add, 'then the worse case scenario is that Mary will end up with a rather special Christmas present.'

Because James has inherited his mother's brains and my barrow-boy instincts, there's no need to repeat anything. We agree to speak again by phone towards the end of the week. I smile across at David and he joins us.

After a few preliminaries about his wife, Sue, and whether they had a good holiday, I can see he's nervous, which has always been David's way of telling me something is worrying him. I try to make it as easy as possible for both of us.

'Are you still thinking of emigrating to Australia?' I ask.

'No,' he replies, 'much as I'd like to, it's near impossible to get on the quota, unless you have a job to go to, or relatives already living there.'

'I suppose I'll have a better chance now I've been to prison,' I suggest, before adding, 'So what *are* you planning to do?'

'Sue and I are thinking of settling in Turkey. We've spent our last few holidays there, and we like the people, the climate and most of all the cost of living.'

'So when would you want to leave?'

'In a couple of months, if that's all right with you, boss?'

I smile and tell him that's just fine. We shake hands like old friends, because that's exactly what we are.

The four of us spend the last thirty minutes together swapping stories as if I wasn't in jail. I think I've made this observation before, but if your friends could be in prison with you, it would be almost bearable.

I place the pens Will smuggled in into my shirt pocket and just hope. I'm sorry to see the boys leave, and it's only their absence that reminds me just how much I love them. The officer who carries out the search checks my mouth, under my tongue, makes me take off my shoes, and then finishes with a Heathrow check. I escape – which means for the next week I'll be able to write with the implement of my choice.

5.00 pm

After supper I convene a board meeting in Sergio's cell. 'The ball is now in your court,' I tell him. 'You've selected the emerald, so we're about to discover if you're a serious player or a mountebank.' He has asked me to use one expression and one word every day that he won't have heard before. He immediately looks up mountebank in his Spanish/English dictionary.

He then stands and formally shakes my hand. 'The ball is now in my court,' he repeats, 'and you're about to find out that despite the circumstances in which we've met, I am not a mountebank.' I want to believe him.

DAY 48   TUESDAY 4 SEPTEMBER 2001

6.11 am

One of the interesting aspects of writing this diary during the day, and correcting the script of volume one in the evening, is being reminded just how horrendous an experience Belmarsh was.

9.00 am

Pottery. Paul gives us a lecture with slides on Rothko, Man Ray, Magritte and Andy Warhol. Several of the prisoners voice an opinion often heard about modern artists, only they put it more bluntly.

'That's fuckin' crap, why would anyone pay good money for that shit? My seven-year-old daughter could knock you up one of those.'

Neither of our tutors, Paul nor Anne, comments; both are professional artists and know only too well that if they could 'knock up one of those', they wouldn't be teaching in prison.

After the lecture Shaun presents me with a pattern for my cell wall – unquestionably influenced by Magritte. It's fun, but I wonder if Locke is capable of reproducing it. I'll have to discuss the problem with my *chef de chantier*, Darren. Will I really be allowed a sun and moon in my room?

DAY 48

2.00 pm

Education. Tuesday afternoon is a bit of a farce. I have to attend an education class to make up the statutory number of lessons required by a part-time worker – £6.50 a week – so end up sitting at the back of the classroom working on this script.

I've asked Wendy Sergeant (Head of the Education Department) if I can teach one lesson a week of creative writing, as I did at Belmarsh. Her latest comment on the subject is that the prisoners don't want another inmate teaching them. I find this unlikely because at least one inmate a day asks me to read and comment on something they've written, so I wonder what the truth really is. I won't bother Wendy again as it's obvious that someone else has made the decision, and she is simply carrying out instructions. In future I'll just sit at the back of the classroom and continue working for myself.

5.00 pm

Board meeting. Sergio reports that he's spoken to his brother again, and all the arrangements are in place. But he has an anxious look on his face.

'What's the problem?' I ask.

'I'm worried about my brother,' he explains. 'He's a civil servant, an academic, not used to the way business is carried out in Colombia. It must have taken a great deal of courage for him to travel to the mountain where no one would give a second thought to killing you for a thousand dollars. Now we want him to hand over ten thousand in cash and then transport the emerald to the airport without any protection.' Sergio pauses. 'I fear for his life.'

My first thought is that Sergio is trying to get off the hook now that he's leaving these shores in a few weeks' time.

'What are you suggesting?' I venture.

'Perhaps it would be wiser to wait until I return to Bogotá, then I can handle the problem personally. I fear for my brother's life,' he repeats.

Once Sergio is back in Bogotá I will have lost all contact with him, not to mention my £200. He has claimed many times during the past three weeks that several prisoners have offered to transfer money to his account in Bogotá in exchange for a regular supply of drugs, but he has always turned them down. Has he in fact accepted every payment? Is that account now in surplus thus guaranteeing him an easy life once he's back in Colombia? However, I feel I am left with no choice but to take the high road.

'If you're in any doubt about your brother's safety,' I tell him, 'let's postpone the sending of the emerald until you return to Bogotá.'

Sergio looks relieved. 'I'll call him tomorrow,' he says, 'and then I'll let you know our decision.'

I close the board meeting because, given the circumstances, there's not a lot more to discuss.

6.00 pm

Exercise. Shaun has finished his preliminary sketch of Darren, and is now making a further attempt at Dale.

As Jimmy and I proceed on our usual circuit (there isn't a lot of choice) we pass a group of three officers who are posted to keep an eye on us. One of them is a young, not unattractive, woman. Jimmy tells me that she has a 'bit of a thing' about Malcolm (ABH, punched a publican) who she will miss when he's transferred to his D-cat prison on Monday.

'The stories I could tell you about Malcolm,' says Jimmy.

'Yes, yes,' I say, my ears pricking up.

'No, no,' says Jimmy. 'I'm not saying a word about that man until I'm sure he's safely ensconced at Latchmere House. He flattened that publican with one punch.' He pauses. 'But ask me again next week.'

9.00 pm

I watch Ian Richardson on BBC 1 playing Dr Bell in a Conan Doyle drama described in *The Times* as the forerunner to Sherlock Holmes. I will never forget his portrayal of the chief whip in Michael Dobbs' excellent *House of Cards*. I've known seven chief whips in my time – Willie Whitelaw, Francis Pym, Humphrey Atkins, John Wakeham, Tim Renton, Peter Brooke, and Richard Ryder – but even their combined talents lacked the Machiavellian skills of Francis Urquhart, under whose gaze I certainly wouldn't have dared to miss a vote.

11.00 pm

I lie awake thinking about Sergio. Is he a liar, just another two-bit con man, or is he genuinely anxious about his brother's safety? Only time will tell.

DAY 49   WEDNESDAY 5 SEPTEMBER 2001

5.51 am

Locke has finished painting my cell, but is nervous about attempting the Magritte pattern Shaun has designed for the wall. Darren, as works manager, agrees that it's far too elaborate, and should be cut down to about half the original, and even then he's not sure I'll get away with it. But as Darren points out, the worst they can do is make us return the paintwork to its original colour – cost, £1. So it's agreed that while I'm away at pottery, the redecorating will begin, and then we'll have to wait and see how the spur officer reacts.

9.00 am

Pottery. Today the class settles down to do a still-life drawing. Anne, our tutor, and former Slade graduate, has taken a lot of trouble in gathering together objects of interest to make the drawing more of a challenge. She has set up in the centre of the room a small card table, and placed over it a cloth with a red and white diamond pattern. On the table she's placed an empty wine bottle, a green vase and a fruit bowl. In the bowl she's carefully arranged a bunch of grapes, a pineapple, three oranges, two apples and a peach. Paul, one of our other tutors, has supplied a cheese board and a lump of Cheddar.

We all sit round the table in a circle and attempt to draw what we see in front of us. Keith (kidnapper), who is sitting next to me, will present the piece as part of his A-level submission. He understands both perspective and shading. I, on the other hand, do not. Anne helpfully points out – to everyone else's amusement – that my peach is bigger than my pineapple.

After an hour, we're given a ten-minute break, when most of the prisoners go off for a quick drag. Shaun and I disappear with Anne into her office to discuss some ideas for a prison landscape which I hope to include in this book. I take up as much of her time as possible, because I can't face another hour of still-life drawing. However, she seems keen to get back and see how the others are progressing.

Anne is a very easy-going person and I can't imagine her losing her temper. But when she walks back into the main room and sees the still-life table, she goes berserk. All that remains of the original offering is two apple cores, the top of a pineapple, three orange skins, a peach stone, a grape stalk with one grape attached and a cheese board with just a few morsels left on it. To be fair, what is left has been artistically arranged, and her pupils are studiously drawing the new composition.

I burst out laughing, and it is only moments before Anne joins in. I am happy to report that Keith's final effort was entered as part of his A level submission, and gained high marks for originality.

2.00 pm

Rugby. Over fifty prisoners turn out for the first training session of the season, which takes place on the main field adjacent to the football pitch. For an hour our coach, Andy Harley, puts us through passing and handling skills, and it soon becomes clear that several prisoners have never played the game before. For the last thirty minutes, the coach selects two sides for a game of touch rugby, which he asks me to referee. He tells me that I had refereed him some years before when a Newmarket XV visited Cambridge.

Because several of the prisoners didn't know the laws of the game, I had to be fairly liberal if I wasn't going to have to blow the whistle every few seconds for some minor infringement. However, I was left with little choice when a large black man threw the ball twenty yards forward, as if he were playing American football. I blew the whistle and awarded the blue side a penalty. He immediately bore down on me, shouting expletives, while the others stood around and watched. I paced ten yards towards his goal line, explaining that in rugby you can't swear at the referee. His language became riper, so I advanced another ten yards, by which time he had been joined by three of his mates who weren't much smaller. Two of the coaches ran quickly onto the field, and Mr Harley explained, 'Jeffrey is right. If you argue with the referee in rugby, it's automatically a penalty, and you'd better get used to it, because when we have our first match next week, a neutral ref will be even stricter.' Many of the prisoners looking on remained silent, as no one was sure what would happen next.

'Sorry, Jeff,' said the big black man, and added, 'it's just that we never played it like that in Brixton.' He then rejoined his team.

When I returned to the block, I went straight to the shower room, and a few minutes later was joined by Jimmy.

'I scored two goals,' he informs me, before adding, 'I've just heard about you and Big Nes.'

'Big Nes?'

'Yeah, Big Nes from Block C. I've managed to go a whole year without speaking to him.'

DAY 49

'Why?' I asked.

'He was Brixton heavyweight champion, and I once saw him knock a prisoner out with a single blow, and no one was sure what the poor bastard had done to annoy him.'

'Oh Christ,' I said, shaking under the shower, 'I'll never be able to go into the exercise yard again.'

'No, no,' said Jimmy, 'Big Nes is telling everyone you're his new friend.'

5.00 pm

I collect my supper from the hotplate, but Sergio avoids any eye contact.

As it's Wednesday, you have to change your sheets, blankets and towels after supper, so I was too preoccupied to go in search of him. Darren popped in while I was making up my bed to attach nine small mirrors to the wall using prison toothpaste as an adhesive. Regulations allow you only one five-by-five-inch mirror, so heaven knows how Darren got his hands on the other eight.

6.00 pm

I go in search of Sergio, and spot him on the phone. I return to my cell thinking he'll probably visit me once he's finished his call . . . he doesn't.

10.00 pm

I'm exhausted and fall asleep fully dressed with the TV still on. Only later do I learn that it is an offence to fall asleep fully dressed, for which you can be put on report.

DAY 50   THURSDAY 6 SEPTEMBER 2001

6.57 am

The cell is at last finished and no longer smells of paint. Locke has run a day and a half over time, which is no more than one would expect from any self-respecting painter and decorator. Darren comes in to pick up my washing, sighs, and declares the new decor reminds him of a 1970s council house. He leaves with his nose in the air and several bundles of washing over his shoulder.

9.00 am

Pottery is cancelled as once a fortnight the prison officers carry out a session of in-house training, which means we're banged up for the rest of the morning. I attempt yesterday's *Times* crossword, and manage to complete three clues – quid, Turgenev and courtier. I can only improve.

12 noon

Lunch. When I go to pick up my meal from the hotplate, Sergio welcomes me with a broad grin, so I assume that after all those phone calls he has some news. However, I won't have a chance to meet up with him until after I've returned from the gym.

2.00 pm

Gym. It's circuit day. I try to keep up with Minnie the traveller, and manage to do ten press-ups to his fifteen, and maintain the same ratio for sit-ups, bench presses, squats, pull ups and back raises, but let's face it, he's only forty-five and in the sixth year of an eleven-year sentence. He's hoping for parole next year.* At the end of the session, Minnie nods. He's a man of few words, and a nod is considered a remarkable gesture for someone he's only known for a month.

5.00 pm

Board meeting. Sergio begins by apologizing for not reporting back last night, but he had to call Bogotá six times and, in the process, went through nineteen phonecards (£38). To fund this, he had to sell his radio, a cassette player and an Adidas tracksuit. I hope I looked suitably guilty.

He tells me that the paperwork for the emerald is now complete (insurance, registration, authentication certificate, export licence and tax) and it's ready to be shipped. His brother, as you will recall, is a senior civil servant and therefore plays everything by the book. He has already told Sergio that he has no intention of losing his job over one small emerald. I feel even more guilty as I listen to the rest of Sergio's Colombian report . . .

---

* He was released in October 2002.

6.00 pm

Darren rushes into my cell. 'A problem,' he announces. Mr Meanwell has just witnessed him opening a registered parcel in reception. It turned out to be a plate and bowl sent in by my son Will. 'Prisoners are not allowed to send in gifts for other inmates, as it might be construed as a bribe, in exchange for drugs or protection.' Darren warns me that Mr Meanwell would be calling for me at some point, and perhaps it might be wiser if I were to go and 'bell the cat'. I shake my head. Meanwell is a wise old bird, and he'll work out that a plate and bowl doesn't constitute a bribe, and in any case, everyone is well aware of my views on drugs. He will also realize that I made no attempt to hide the gift. Will's name was printed all across the box, together with a compliment slip from my PA, which would allow Mr Meanwell to place the offending plate and bowl with the rest of my confiscated kit downstairs if he was at all suspicious. Like Nelson, Meanwell knows when to turn a blind eye.

6.15 pm

Exercise. It's the final evening outing. The nights are drawing in and we won't be allowed out again after six. I perambulate around the yard with Steve (not librarian Steve) who, because he's a D-cat prisoner, has spent the day out with his family. I ask him if he enjoyed the experience (9 am to 3 pm).

'Very much,' he replied, 'but only thanks to some help from the police.'

'The police?' I repeat.

He explains. One of the activities Steve most misses while he's in jail is a regular swim, so whenever he has a day release, he and the family go off to the local swimming pool. On this occasion they left their Ford in the municipal car park, and took the children to the pool. When they returned, his wife couldn't find her car keys, until one of the children spotted them on the back seat. Steve ran all the way to the nearest police station explaining his dilemma, exacerbated by the fact that if he failed to return to Wayland by three o'clock, he would automatically lose his D-cat status. The police happily broke into his car, and even phoned Wayland to confirm what happened. Steve arrived back at the front gate with ten minutes to spare.

DAY 51   FRIDAY 7 SEPTEMBER 2001

5.39 am

I have now been a resident of Wayland for a month, and Sergio will return to Colombia in a couple of weeks' time. So with a bit of luck he'll be deported around the same time as I'm being transferred to a D-cat. But will I also be in possession of an emerald?

9.00 am

Gym. Friday is special needs group, and my four new friends Alex, Robbie, Les and Paul shake hands with me as they come through the gate. Again all four display different talents during the training session. Les can now complete 1,650 metres on the rowing machine in ten minutes, but can only manage one mile an hour on the treadmill, whereas Paul can do five miles an hour on the running machine, but can't catch a ball. Robbie can catch anything, but hates all the machines, so only does weight training.

The instructors rightly tell us to play to their strengths, which results in much clapping and laughter, along with a huge sense of achievement.

DAY 51

Jimmy handles them better than anyone. He remembers all their names (over twenty came this morning) and they feel he's a real friend. He'd make a great PE teacher, but I have a feeling that once he's released the lure of easy money may be more attractive. He says he'll never deal in drugs again, but I wonder.

6.00 pm

Exercise. Cancelled because it's raining.

7.00 pm

Sergio calls his brother in Bogotá, but the line is engaged.

7.05 pm

Sergio comes to my cell and continues his tutorial on the history of Colombia. The political system is not unlike that of the United States with a president, vice-president, Senate and Congress. However, there are two big differences: the president and vice-president have to come from different parties, one conservative, one liberal – Colombia's idea of democracy – whereas in truth the president has all the power. The other big difference is that even a senator requires four bodyguards. Sergio tells me that one presidential candidate had forty bodyguards when he delivered a speech in Bogotá, and was still assassinated.

7.20 pm

Sergio tries his brother again. Still engaged.

7.23 pm

Sergio continues his lecture, explaining that the violence in his country makes it necessary for any presidential candidate to have an accommodation with the guerrillas or the Mafia or the army, or all three. We sometimes forget how fortunate we are in Britain. Our politicians only have to deal with the trade unions, the CBI – and Messrs Paxman and Humphreys.

7.35 pm

Sergio tries his brother again. Still engaged.

7.40 pm

According to Sergio, the civil service remains the only untainted profession. Although his brother is an adviser to several ministers, he doesn't need a bodyguard because it is accepted that he will never take a bribe from either the Mafia, the guerrillas or the army. The countryside, he assures me, is beautiful and the beaches that face both the Pacific and the Atlantic rival any that can be found in America or Europe. And as for the women . . .

DAY 52   SATURDAY 8 SEPTEMBER 2001

6.01 am

Since the age of twenty-six, I've been lucky enough to organize my own life, so having to follow the same routine day in and day out, weekends included, is enough to make one go stark raving bonkers. If I weren't writing this diary, and Sergio didn't exist, they would have had to put me in a straitjacket long before now and cart me off to the nearest asylum.

9.00 am

Gym. I put myself through a tough workout, and what makes it even tougher is that I'm surrounded by prisoners a third of my age. At the end of the session I climb onto the scales, to find I've put on a pound in the last week. I'll have to cut down on my chocolate intake. One of the many disadvantages of being locked up in a cell for hour upon hour is that sometimes you eat simply because there is nothing else to do (this is one of the reasons prisoners experiment with drugs, and addicts need a regular fix). In future I must show more self-control. If I don't buy it, I can't eat it.

Between each exercise, ten minutes on the treadmill, the

rower and the bicycle, I walk a complete circuit of the gym to get my breath back. By now I know most of the prisoners and the workouts they do, and usually acknowledge or encourage them as I stroll by. As I pass Jimmy he flexes his muscles, and describes himself as a gay icon; I'm seen by the other inmates as the geriatric icon.

Today I spot a six-foot-three West Indian of about twenty stone who's lifting massive weights on his own, so I stop to watch him.

'What are you fuckin' staring at?' he demands, once he's put the weights down.

'Just watching,' I reply.

'Then fuck off. I know you talk to everyone else, but you don't fuckin' talk to me.' I can't stop laughing, which doesn't seem to please him and has the officers on edge. 'Do you want your fuckin' head knocked off?' he asks.

'I don't think so, Ellis.' He looks surprised that I know his name. 'Not if you're hoping to be out of here in two weeks' time.' He looks even more surprised that I know when he's due to be released. He grunts, turns his back on me and lifts 210 kilos. In prison, what you know is every bit as important as who you know.

2.00 pm

As I cross the corridor to join Darren in his cell for a game of backgammon, I spot Sergio on the phone. He's holding a stack of £2 phonecards in his left hand; by now he must have traded everything he owns. Lately, his cell looks as if the bailiffs have paid a visit.

After three games, I return to my cell in possession of another Mars bar. If I am going to lose weight, I'm going to have to start losing at backgammon. I glance to my left to see Sergio furiously beckoning me.

'I need another phonecard,' he says desperately. I remove the one I always carry in the back pocket of my jeans and hand it over. He smiles. I return to my cell, sit at my desk and wait, sensing a board meeting is imminent.

2.34 pm

Sergio walks in, pushes the door to (if anyone enters your cell, officer or inmate, it's against regulations to lock yourself in) and turns on the TV – a sign that means he doesn't want to be overheard. He takes his usual place on the end of the bed, as befits the managing director. He opens his A4 pad.

'The stone takes off,' he checks his watch, 'in a couple of hours.' He can't resist a huge grin as he keeps me waiting. I nod. If I were to speak, it would only hold up the inevitable repetition of the entire conversation he and his brother have just held. And who can blame him? However, I'll skip the next forty minutes and give you a precis of what has caused such a big grin.

Sergio's brother has in fact completed all the paperwork and booked the tiny package onto a Lufthansa flight that leaves Bogotá for Heathrow via Frankfurt in two hours' time (10.30 am in Bogotá, 4.30 pm at Wayland). He has faxed all the relevant details to my office in London, so they'll know when and where to pick up the gem. Sergio pauses at this point and waits for some well-earned praise. He goes on to confirm that the emerald has come from the Muzo mining district, famous for the quality of its stones. It's 3.3 carats, and cost $9,000 (mountain price). Now all we can do is wait until I find out what value is placed on the emerald by my gemmologist. Sergio looks up from his notes, and adds that his brother would like confirmation that the fax has arrived in my office.

'Right now,' I ask, 'or when you've completed your report?' because I can see that he's only about halfway through the pages that are covered in his neat Spanish hand. He considers this for a moment, and then says, 'No, I'll finish first.

'The second piece of news,' continues Sergio, turning another page, unable to suppress an even broader grin, 'is that Liana' – his former school friend – 'has tracked down four Boteros in private hands. In private hands,' he repeats with considerable emphasis. 'And they could be for sale. She will send the details to your office some time next week.' He checks his diary. 'That will give you twelve days to evaluate them. Evaluate,' he repeats. 'Is that the correct word?' I nod, impressed. 'By the time you have decided on a realistic price, I will be back in Colombia and can take over negotiations.' He closes the A4 pad.

'I'd better call my son,' I say, aware the ball is back in my court. 'Any units left on my phonecard?' I ask, returning to the real world.

3.17 pm

I call James on his mobile and ask where he is.

'In the car, Dad, but I'll be back at the flat in about fifteen minutes.' I put the phone down. Three units gone – mobiles gobble units. I return to my cell to tell Sergio I won't know if James has received the fax for another fifteen minutes. This gives Sergio enough time to repeat the highlights of his earlier triumph not unlike replays of Owen's hat-trick against Germany.

3.35 pm

I call Jamie at the flat and ask him if he's received the fax.

'Yes,' he replies, 'it arrived forty minutes ago.'

'And does it give you all the details you need?'

'Yes,' he replies.

I put the phone down. Sergio leaves me as he has to report for his job behind the hotplate. Although he too has to return to the real world, that grin just doesn't leave his face.

4.30 pm

Exercise. Darren and I are joined by Jason (conspiracy to blackmail) on our afternoon power walk. We pass Shaun who is sketching Jules, with whom I shared a cell for the first two weeks. He's now finished Darren and Dale and once he's completed Jules, he'll only have Jimmy to do, so he should have a full house by the end of the week.

'Why do I have this feeling,' asks Darren, 'that you consider the Prison Service has only one purpose, and that is to cater for your every need?'

'That's neither accurate nor fair,' I protest. 'I've tried to organize my entire life around the schedule the Prison Service demands. It makes it twice as difficult to carry out my usual routines, but it has put another perspective on the unforgiving minute.'

'I wish I could work the system,' says Jason. 'They had me in for an MDT (mandatory drugs test) this afternoon, à la Ann Widdecombe.'

'Will it prove positive?' I ask.

'No chance, I'm in the clear. What a nerve,' he adds, 'suggesting that it was "on the grounds of reasonable suspicion".'

'Knowing your past record,' says Darren – well aware that Jason occasionally dabbles in heroin – 'how can you be so confident you're in the clear?'

'Simple,' Jason replies. 'For the past three days I've been drinking more water than Jeffrey. I must have been up peeing at least seven times every night.'

5.40 pm

We're banged up for fourteen hours. After I've checked over the day's script, I turn to my letters. I am particularly touched by a missive from Gillian Shephard. She describes herself as 'your temporary MP'. She offers her support and goes on to point out that, 'No one can suggest I'm after your vote. After all, members of the House of Lords, convicted prisoners and lunatics are not entitled to a vote.' She concludes, 'There's only one category left for you to fulfil, Jeffrey.'

10.00 pm

I climb into bed and start to think about an aeroplane that's already halfway across the Atlantic on its way to Heathrow. In its massive hold there is a tiny package, no larger than an Oxo cube, and inside a tiny emerald that will either be on its way back to Bogotá in a few days' time, or hanging on my family's Christmas tree come December.

DAY 53   SUNDAY 9 SEPTEMBER 2001

5.39 am

The strangest thing happened last night, and I'm going to have to follow it up today. However, in order for you to be able to understand its significance, I'll first have to explain the layout of the enhanced spur on A block. The spur is L-shaped, with fourteen cells on each sprig. If I look out of the window to my left, I can see about five of the windows on the adjoining sprig.

Around eight yesterday evening, just after I'd finished writing for the day, I rose from my desk to draw the curtains, when I noticed a woman officer of about twenty-five years of age (I'd better not describe her in detail) chatting to a prisoner through his window. I wouldn't have given it a second thought – if she hadn't still been there an hour later ... now I'm unable to tell you any more at the moment, because I was banged up at five forty last night, and will not be let out until eight fifteen this morning. I shall then approach the oracle of all knowledge, Darren, and report back to you tomorrow. I have a feeling he'll know both the officer and the prisoner and – more importantly – be able to throw some light on their relationship.

9.00 am

Jimmy, Carl, Jules, Shane and I go across to the changing rooms for the football match against Lakenheath. After last Sunday's victory, and two good training sessions during the week, the team are buoyed up and ready for the encounter.

In my role as match reporter, I look around the benches and check to make sure I know the names of every team member. The players are becoming quite nervous, and start jumping up and down on the spot as they wait for the arrival of our coach to deliver his pep talk. Kevin Lloyd appears a few moments later, a look of despondency on his face.

'I'm sorry, lads,' he says, 'but the game's off.' A voluble groan goes round the changing room. 'Two of the opposition,' Kevin continues, 'failed to bring any form of ID with them, so we couldn't let them through the gates. I would have accepted credit cards, but they couldn't even supply those. I am sorry,' Kevin repeats, and there's no doubt he's as disappointed as we are.

While the others go off for a further training session, I have to return to my cell.

11.00 am

I call Mary, who brings me up to date on the reinstatement of my D-cat. 'KPMG's report is progressing slowly,' she tells me, 'and the police haven't even decided if they want to interview you.' Although the whole exercise is taking longer than she had anticipated, Mary says there is no reason to believe that they will find Ms Nicholson's accusations anything other than spurious.

I suggest that she goes ahead with the Christmas parties that

DAY 53

we always hold in December and let Will and James act as co-hosts. I tell her to invite everyone who has stood firm and ignore the fair-weather friends (who have in fact turned out to be very small in number). I add that if I'm in a D-cat open prison by Christmas, I'll call up in the middle of the party and deliver a festive message over the intercom.

4.30 pm

I'm just about to leave for exercise when the spur officer tells me I'm required urgently in the SO's office. The word 'urgently' surprises me, as I haven't heard it used for the past seven weeks.

I join Mr King in his office, and am introduced to a female officer I've never seen before. Am I at last to meet the governor? No. The officer's name is Sue Maiden and she explains that she's part of the prison's security team. She then tells me that it has been reported to her that Ellis, who resides on B block, was abusive to me in the gym yesterday. I repeat exactly what took place. She then asks me if I want special protection.

'Certainly not,' I reply. 'That's the last thing I need.' She looks relieved.

'I had to ask,' she explains.

'That's all I need,' I repeat. 'You only have to read the story in the *Sunday Mirror* this morning about phonecards to see what the press would make of that.'

'Understood, but we'll still have to speak to Ellis.'

'Fine, but not at my request,' I make clear. She seems to accept this proviso, and I depart to find the barred gate that leads out on to the exercise yard has already been bolted, leaving me locked inside and unable to take my daily walk around the yard.

5.00 pm

I spend the forty minutes with Sergio in his cell. He tells me that there is only one recognized carrier willing to fly in and out of Bogotá, and then only on a Thursday, Saturday and Sunday. Sergio mentions that it's not easy to attract holidaymakers to a country where there are forty murders a day in the capital alone.

He uses the rest of exercise time to give me a geography lesson. I am shown in Darren's *Times* atlas (he's playing backgammon) where the emerald mountains are situated, as well as the extensive oil fields in the valleys to the east. I also discover that both the Andes and the Amazon make entrances and exits through Colombia.

6.00 pm

I drop into Darren's cell to have a blackcurrant cordial and watch him play a game of backgammon with Jimmy. He tells me that my meeting with the security officer was timed so that I wouldn't be able to go out into the exercise yard, as they felt it might be wise for me to cool it a little. Darren seems to know everything that's going on, and I take the opportunity to tell him about my nocturnal sightings.

Darren laughs. 'You're a peeping Tom,' he says. 'That has to be Malcolm. Macho Malcolm.'

'He's even more irresistible than me,' chips in Jimmy.

'Do I sense a good story for the diary?' I ask tentatively.

'Half a dozen,' says Darren, 'but not tonight because we're just about to be banged up.' He can't hide his pleasure at the thought of keeping me waiting for another few hours.

DAY 53

8.00 pm

Once I'm banged up, I start making extensive notes for my phone call to Alison, who returns from New Zealand tomorrow. I then turn to *Hamlet*. I am resolved to read, or reread, the entire works of Shakespeare – thirty-seven plays – by the time they transfer me to an open prison. If I succeed, I'll move on to the Sonnets.

After a couple of acts, I switch on the TV to watch the unforgettable John Le Mesurier in *Dad's Army*. What a distinguished career he had, making a virtue of letting other people take centre stage. Not something I've ever been good at.

DAY 54   MONDAY 10 SEPTEMBER 2001

5.51 am

Tomorrow and tomorrow and tomorrow . . .*

Tomorrow, I will need to book a call at seven in the evening
with my son James, to find out if the emerald has arrived. I can't
contact him today because on Monday we're banged up at five-
thirty, and he'll still be at work in the City.

Tomorrow ... Macho Malcolm leaves for his D-cat prison,
and neither Darren nor Jimmy are willing to breathe a word
about his sex life until he's off the premises. However, I *can*
report that the woman officer who was spotted outside Malcolm's window was today seen walking down the corridor with
him towards his cell. But this is the stuff of rumours; tomorrow I
will be able to give you the facts as reported by Darren and
Jimmy. However, Darren did let slip that three women were
involved. He knows only too well such a hint will keep me
intrigued for another night.

Tomorrow ...

As for today, I rise a few minutes before six and write for two
hours.

---

* When I originally wrote these words, I had no idea how portentous tomorrow
would turn out to be.

DAY 54

9.00 am

Pottery. I take a grapefruit into art class, and an empty jar of marmalade for Keith (kidnapping) as part of another still life he's drawing for his A level course. Keith didn't even take up painting until he was sent to prison. When he comes up for parole in six months' time, he will leave, at the age of forty-six, with an A level. Much credit must go to Anne and Paul, who are every bit as proud of this achievement as Keith himself.

Keith tells me how sorry he was to read about my mother's death, and goes on to say that he was in prison when his wife died of breast cancer at the age of thirty-nine. He then adds the poignant comment, 'I shall not mourn her death until after I've been released.'

Shaun (forgery, artist) confirms that he's given up on Dale, and will now concentrate on Jules, Steve and Jimmy. We discuss how he'll deal with the arrival on Wednesday of his cache of special drawing paper, oils, chalks and pencils without the other prisoners becoming aware of what I'm up to. We don't want to get our smuggler into any trouble, and we certainly don't need any other inmates to feel envious.

Envy is even more prevalent in prisons than it is in the outside world, partly because all emotions are heightened in such a hot-house atmosphere, and partly because any little privilege afforded to one, however slight, seems so unfair to others who are not treated in the same way.

I spend the remainder of the class reading a book on the lives of the two great female Impressionists, Marie Laurencin and Berthe Morisot.

2.00 pm

Gym. Once again I complete my programme in the allocated hour. Just to give you an update on my progress, when I first arrived at Wayland four weeks ago, I managed 1,800 metres on the rowing machine, and today I passed 2,200 for the first time. When, and if, I ever get to a D-cat establishment, I can only hope they have a well-equipped gym.

3.42 pm

Mr Chapman unlocks my cell door to let me know that Mr Carlton-Boyce wants to see me.

Mr Carlton-Boyce, who seems to be the governor on my case, tells me that he can do nothing about the reinstatement of my D-cat until the police confirm that they will not be going ahead with any enquiry concerning the Simple Truth appeal.

'However,' he adds, 'once that confirmation comes through, we will transfer you to an open prison as quickly as possible. I am still receiving a pile of letters from the public every day,' he adds, 'but they just don't understand that my hands are tied.' I accept this, but point out that it's been six weeks, and the police haven't even interviewed me. He nods, and then asks me if I have any other problems. I say no, although I have a feeling he's referring to Ellis and the gym incident.

5.30 pm

I call Alison. I make an appointment to speak to Jonathan Lloyd, my agent, at five tomorrow and my son James at seven. I have to book 'time calls' because, as you will recall, no one can phone in.

DAY 54

5.45 pm

Banged up for another fourteen hours, so once I've gone over my script, I turn to my letters, one of which is from a journalist.

How flattering the press can be when they want something.

9.00 pm

I watch David Starkey present the first of an engrossing four-part series on the six wives of Henry VIII. I had no idea that Catherine of Aragon had been made regent and conducted a war against the Scots (Flodden 1513) while Henry was away fighting his own battles in France, or that they were married for over thirty years, and of course would have remained together until death if she had only produced a son. More please, Dr Starkey. I can't wait to learn about Anne Boleyn next week; even I know that she was the mother of Elizabeth I, but not a lot more.

10.00 pm

The lead story on the news is that John Prescott's retaliatory punch during the election campaign is to be referred to the CPS. Over the past few weeks several inmates have pointed out that they are serving sentences from six months to three years for punching someone after they had been attacked, so they're looking forward to the deputy prime minister joining us. I have little doubt that the CPS will sweep the whole incident under the carpet, I say when I raise the subject with Darren. 'They didn't in your case,' he remarks.

True, but it won't go unnoticed by the public that we can

expect two levels of justice in Britain as long as New Labour are in power. I just can't see Mr Prescott arriving at Belmarsh in two sweatboxes. Perhaps I do the CPS an injustice.

Tomorrow and tomorrow and tomorrow . . .

DAY 55   TUESDAY 11 SEPTEMBER 2001

5.39 am

I suspect that Tuesday September 11th 2001 will be etched on the memories of everyone in the free world as among the blackest days in history. But I shall still report it as it unfolded for me, in time sequence, although aware that my earlier reportage may appear frivolous.

9.40 am

Pottery is cancelled because Anne's car has broken down, so all the prisoners in the art class have to return to their cells (the first irony). Back on A block, everyone on my spur is shaking hands with Malcolm, who is about to be transferred to a D-cat. He comes to my cell to say farewell, and hopes that I will be joining him soon, as he knows Spring Hill is also my first choice.

'When are Group 4 collecting you?' I ask.

'They aren't,' he replies. 'Now I'm in a D-cat and past my FLED,* I can drive myself over to Aylesbury, and as long as I've checked in by three this afternoon, no one will give a damn.'

---

* FLED – Facility Licence Eligibility Date, one quarter of your sentence.

No sooner has Malcolm left the wing, than Jimmy slips into my cell. 'I'm ready to talk now,' he says.

Jimmy and Malcolm are both D-cats (Jimmy remains at Wayland because his home is nearby) and are the only two inmates at Wayland allowed to work outside the prison walls every day. Both of them have a job maintaining the grounds beyond the perimeter fence during the week, and at an animal sanctuary on Saturday mornings. The sanctuary is a voluntary project, which concentrates on helping animals in distress. The work ranges from assisting lame beasts to walk or birds to fly, to having to bury them when they die.

Every Saturday morning at the sanctuary, Jimmy and Malcolm join several volunteers from the local village. Among them one lady who has left Malcolm in no doubt how she feels about him – Malcolm has the rugged looks of a matinee idol, and possesses an inordinate amount of charm.

One of the tasks none of the volunteers relish is having to bury dead animals, and Percy the hedgehog was no exception. Everyone was surprised when the lady in question stepped forward and volunteered to bury Percy. Malcolm, gallant as ever, quickly agreed to accompany her into the forest that bordered the sanctuary.

Armed with spades, they disappeared into the thicket. Forty-five minutes later they reappeared but, Jimmy noticed, minus their spades.

'Where's your spade, mate?' demanded Jimmy.

'I knew there was something else we were meant to do,' Malcolm blurted out. They both charged back into the forest, and Malcolm returned only just in time to be escorted back to the prison.

Jimmy goes on to tell me that Malcolm left Wayland just in time, because one of the ladies who served behind the counter at family visits has also just signed up to join the group on Saturdays at the animal sanctuary. Not to mention the female officer who I saw standing outside his cell window for an hour two nights ago, who is now thinking of applying for a transfer . . .

'God knows,' says Jimmy, 'what Malcolm will get up to in a D-cat where the regime is far more relaxed.'

'Is he married?' I ask.

'Oh yeah,' Jimmy replies. 'Happily.'

1.17 pm

I am sitting on the end of my bed reading *The Times* when Darren bursts in without knocking – most unlike him.

'Switch on your TV,' he says without explanation, 'they're running it on every channel.'

Together we watch the horrors unfold in New York. I assume that the first plane must have been involved in some tragic accident, until we both witness a second jet flying into the other tower of the World Trade Center. To begin with, I feel the commentator's comparison with Pearl Harbor is somewhat exaggerated. But later, when I realize the full extent of the devastation and loss of life, I am less sure. The reporters have already moved on to asking, 'Who is responsible?'

Although I am mesmerized by this vile piece of history as it continues to unfold, prison timetables cannot be altered, whatever is taking place in the rest of the world. If I don't report to the gym by three fifteen, they will come in search of me.

3.15 pm

Much of the talk in the gym is of the carnage in New York and its consequences, although several of the prisoners continue their bench presses, oblivious to what's taking place in the outside world. As soon as the hour is up, I rush back to my cell to find that the Pentagon has been hit by a third domestic carrier, and a fourth commercial plane thought to have been heading for the White House has crashed just outside Pennsylvania.

4.30 pm

For several hours, I sit glued to the television. Among the snippets of news offered between the continual replays of the two planes crashing into the twin towers is a statement by William Hague; he has postponed the announcement of who will be the next leader of the Conservative Party as a mark of respect to the American people.

The prime minister cancels his speech to the TUC in Brighton and hurries back to Downing Street, where he makes a statement fully supporting President Bush, and describing terrorism as the new world evil.

7.00 pm

The sight of innocent people jumping out of those towers and the voices of passengers trapped on a domestic flight talking to their next of kin on mobile phones will be, for me, the enduring memory of this evil day. Calling my agent and my son James was to have been the highlight of my day. It now seems somewhat irrelevant.

DAY 56   WEDNESDAY 12 SEPTEMBER 2001

5.44 am

Yesterday was dominated by the news from America, and what retaliation George W. Bush might take.

Tony Blair seized the initiative by calling a press conference at No. 10 for 2 pm, which would be seen by the citizens of New York just as they were waking. I don't want to appear cynical but, at the end of the press conference, when the prime minister agreed to take questions, did you notice who he selected from a packed audience of journalists? The BBC (Andrew Marr), ITV (John Sergeant), CNN (Robin Oakley), Channel 4 (Eleanor Goodman), *The Times* (Philip Webster) and the *Sun* (Trevor Kavanagh). I sense Alastair Campbell's skills very much in evidence: only the major television companies and two Murdoch newspapers. However, to be fair, by recalling Parliament, Blair looks like the leading statesman in Europe, and that on the day when the Tory party are planning to announce their new leader.

9.00 am

Life goes on at Wayland, so I report to the art room for my pottery class. Our clandestine accomplice has successfully smuggled in the special materials that Shaun needs to complete his art work for this volume.

11.15 am

I call Alison at the office for an update. She tells me that the pressure has shifted onto KPMG to deliver an interim report, so as not to keep me waiting until they've completed the full investigation which apparently now includes some accusations Ms Nicholson has made against the Red Cross which have nothing to do with me. Can't spare any more units, as I have to speak to James tonight, so I say goodbye.

2.00 pm

Football. Wayland's match against RAF Marham is, to my surprise, still on. Not that I expect there would have been many fighter pilots in the visitors' team. We lose 4–3, despite Jimmy's scoring two goals. Three of our team receive red cards, so Wayland ended up with only eight players on the field, having led 3–2 at half-time. By the way, all three players deserved to be sent off.

As soon as I return to my cell, I switch on the TV.

4.00 pm

Most of the Muslim world are swearing allegiance to America, as they must all be fearful of retaliation. Yasser Arafat even gives blood to prove his solidarity with the citizens of New York. The prime minister continues to underline his support for the United States, as he considers the atrocities in New York to be an attack on the democratic world. I suspect he views this as his Falklands. Let's hope it's not his Vietnam.

DAY 56

6.00 pm

After supper Sergio convenes a board meeting. Item No. 1, he confirms that the suitcase and contents have been delivered to his friend in north London. Item No. 2. The emerald has arrived in London, with all the correct paperwork completed. Item No. 3. A colleague of his brother's will be flying into London on Saturday, bringing with him the gold necklace, a catalogue *raisonné* of Botero and four photos of Botero oils that are for sale. He pauses and waits for my reaction. I smile. It all sounds too good to be true.

7.00 pm

I phone James. He tells me that he's tired; he's just started his new job in the City. Because of the upheaval in the American market they expect him to be at his desk by 7 am, and he doesn't leave the office until after 7 pm. However, he confirms over the phone that the emerald has arrived, so out of curiosity I ask him what it looks like.

'It looks magnificient, Dad,' is his simple reply. 'But I've no idea if it's worth ten thousand dollars.'

'When are you hoping to see the expert?'

'Sometime this weekend.'

I don't ask any more questions as I wish to save my remaining units for Mary.

Quite a lot seems to be happening this weekend. Mary will visit Wayland on Friday. Liana will have news of the Botero paintings on Saturday. Sergio's friend flies into London on Sunday, by which time James should have a realistic valuation of the emerald. I only wish I could read Monday's diary now. Don't even think about it.

8.00 pm

All the news programmes are replaying footage from every angle of the American passenger jets flying into the twin towers of the World Trade Center in New York. All the commentators are in no doubt that the US will seek some form of revenge, once they can identify the culprit. Who can blame them? It's going to take a very big man to oversee this whole operation. President Kennedy proved to be such a man when he was faced with the Cuban crisis. I only hope that George W. Bush is of the same mettle.

DAY 57   THURSDAY 13 SEPTEMBER 2001

6.03 am

It was a clear cold night, and for the first time two flimsy blankets were not enough to keep me warm. I had to lie very still if I was not to freeze. It reminded me of being back at boarding school. As two blankets are the regulation issue, I shall have to speak to Darren about the problem. I'm pretty confident he will have a reserve stock.

8.15 am

I watch breakfast television while eating my cornflakes. The news coming out of Washington is that the State Department seems convinced that it was, as has already been widely reported, Osama bin Laden who orchestrated the terrorist attacks. We must now wait and see how George W. Bush plans to retaliate. The president's description of the terrorists as 'folks' hasn't filled the commentators with confidence. Rudy Giuliani, the Mayor of New York, on the other hand, is looking more like a world statesman every day. When the report switches from Washington to New York, I am surprised to observe a pall of smoke still hanging over the city. It's only when the cameras pan down onto the rubble that one is made fully aware of just how long it will be before that city's physical scars can be healed.

9.00 am

We're banged up for an hour owing to officers' staff training.

10.00 am

Pottery. I make my way quickly across to the art class as I need to see Shaun, and find out if he now has all the art materials he needs. I'm disappointed to find that he's not around, so I end up reading a book on the life of Picasso, studying in particular *Guernica* which he painted in support of his countrymen at the time of the Spanish Civil War. I know it's a masterpiece, but I desperately need someone like Brian Sewell to explain to me why.

2.00 pm

Gym. Completed my full programme, and feel fitter than I have done for years.

6.21 pm

Tagged onto the end of the news is an announcement that Iain Duncan Smith has been elected as the new leader of the Conservative Party. He won by a convincing margin of 155,935 (61 per cent) to 100,864 (39 per cent) for Kenneth Clarke. A far better turnout than I had expected. Having spent years trying to convince my party that we should trust our members to select the leader, the 79 per cent turnout gives me some satisfaction. However, I would have to agree with Michael Brown, a former Conservative MP who is now a journalist with the *Independent*: a year ago you could have got odds of a hundred to one against a man who hadn't served in either Margaret Thatcher's or John Major's governments – at any level – ending up as leader of the Tory party in 2001.

10.00 pm

I watch a special edition of *Question Time*, chaired by David Dimbleby. I only hope the audience wasn't a typical cross-section of British opinion, because I was horrified by how many people were happy to condemn the Americans, and seemed to have no sympathy for the innocent people who had lost their lives at the hands of terrorists.

My feelings went out to Philip Lader, the popular former American ambassador, as he found himself having to defend his country's foreign policy.

I fall asleep, angry.

DAY 58   FRIDAY 14 SEPTEMBER 2001

6.17 am

Today is one of those days when I particularly wish I were not in jail. I would like to be in the gallery of the House of Commons following the emergency debate on the atrocities in America, and attending the memorial service at St Paul's.

12 noon

Watching television this afternoon, I find myself agreeing with almost everything the prime minister says in his speech to the House. Iain Duncan Smith responds in a dignified way, leaving the PM in no doubt that the Opposition is, to quote IDS, 'shoulder to shoulder' on this issue. It is left to George Galloway and Tam Dalyell to express contrary views, which they sincerely hold. I suspect it would take a nuclear weapon to land on their constituencies – with Osama bin Laden's signature scribbled across it – before they would be willing to change their minds.

The service at St Paul's sees the British at their best and, like Diana, Princess of Wales' funeral, it strikes exactly the right note, not least by the service opening with the American national anthem and closing with our own.

I am pleased to see Phil Lader sitting amongst the congregation. But it is George Carey, the Archbishop of Canterbury, who rises to the occasion. He delivers an address that leaves no one in any doubt how he feels about the terrorists, but also expresses the view that this is a time for cool heads to make shrewd judgements, rather than macho remarks demanding immediate retaliation.

2.00 pm

Visit. Mary is among the first through the door into the visitors' room.

Her news is not good, and she doesn't try to pretend otherwise. KPMG are going at a snail's pace, making it clear that they have no interest in my plight, and will deliver their report when they are good and ready. They are hoping to interview me on Monday week, so it looks as if I'll be stuck at Wayland for at least another month. I feel sure that is not what Sir Nicholas Young, the CEO of the Red Cross, intended when he instigated an internal enquiry, even if it will delight Emma Nicholson. Mary has so obviously done everything she can to expedite matters, but, as she says, it's an accountant's duty to leave no piece of paper unturned.

We discuss our appeal. Mary describes it as *our* appeal, partly, I think, because she was so offended by Mr Justice Potts aiding and abetting Mrs Peppiatt when she was in the witness box, while in my view not affording Mary the same courtesy when she was put through a similar ordeal.

We talk about the boys, how admirably they are coping in the circumstances, and the fact that Will is desperate to see me before he returns to New York. Thank God he wasn't in Manhattan this week. Mary reports that my adopted sister, Elizabeth, is alive and well. Elizabeth had been at work in the city when she heard the explosion and looked out of her window to see the flames belching from the World Trade Center.

There is a restrained announcement over the intercom asking all visitors to leave. Where did the time go? I feel guilty about Mary. I've been unable to hide my disappointment about KPMG's lack of urgency. She couldn't have been more supportive during this terrible time in my life, and heaven knows what state I would be in without her love and friendship.

DAY 59   SATURDAY 15 SEPTEMBER 2001

9.00 am

I call David and ask him to drive to Sale in Cheshire on Monday and pick up a package which is being flown in from Colombia that morning.

10.00 am

No gym on Saturday, so I make sure I'm standing by the gate when exercise is called. To my surprise Dale is seated in the corner of the yard having his portrait finished. As I pass, he mumbles something about how much trouble he would have been in had he failed to show up two weekends in a row. When I return to my cell after forty-five minutes' hard walking, Darren tells me that we probably covered about three miles. I push open my heavy door to find my cell is spotless. The room has been swept, cleaned and the floor polished by Darren's latest recruit, all for £1. No problems with the minimum wage at Wayland, especially when you can only pay in Mars bars, tobacco or, if it's a big deal, a phonecard.

4.00 pm

Mr Meanwell calls me into his office to let me know that an envelope containing the rules of backgammon has been opened and sent down to reception. It will not be returned to me until I leave Wayland, as the item is on the prohibited list.

'How can the rules of backgammon be on the prohibited list?' I ask.

'The rules came in book form,' he explains, and shrugs his shoulders.

'If they had been in a magazine, could I have had them?' I enquire.

He nods.

6.00 pm

Early bang up. I channel hop so I can keep watching the latest news from Manhattan. I am moved by the sight of the New Yorkers on the streets applauding their firemen as they drive back and forth to the World Trade Center. Americans have a tremendous sense of patriotism and awareness of the country they belong to. It must have been the same in Britain during the last war.

DAY 60   SUNDAY 16 SEPTEMBER 2001

12 noon

Not a lot to report except Sergio is nervous about leaving. He will be deported in twelve days' time and we haven't yet received a valuation for the emerald. He's also waiting to hear about the second package which contains the gold necklace, and can't wait to see the photographs of the Boteros, as well as the catalogue *raisonné*.

I spend a long time reading the papers, and feel the coverage of all that has taken place in America this week elicited the very highest standards of journalism from the British press, not always the case on a Sunday.

DAY 61   MONDAY 17 SEPTEMBER 2001

6.19 am

The news is still all about New York, where Mayor Giuliani appears to be emulating his hero, Mayor La Guardia. Everything had gone wrong for Rudy Giuliani this year. He stood down from the Senate race against Hillary Clinton when he was diagnosed with cancer, and he then moved his mistress into Gracie Mansion to face the wrath of his popular wife and the Big Apple's press; in fact to quote the *New York Times*, 'he seems to have lost the plot'. And then, without warning, the city he loves is attacked by terrorists and all the talents boredom disguises suddenly return.

When I stood for Mayor of London, I spent a week in New York shadowing Giuliani as he went about his daily work, and quickly discovered that he has real power and a real budget to back it up. The truth is that Giuliani runs New York in a way Ken Livingstone can never hope to govern London. Tony Blair's dream of emulating the Americans with mayors in all our major cities would have been admirable, if only he allowed the mayor to be backed up with finance and executive power. Livingstone can huff and puff, but in the end only Blair can blow the house down.

DAY 61

9.00 am

Pottery. Out of boredom I begin, to Anne's surprise, to work on a flowerpot. Or that is what I've told my fellow inmates it's going to be. First you take the putty, run a circle of steel through it to cut off a smaller chunk and then roll it out to produce a long thin worm-like shape. You then twist the long thin worm into a circle and several long worms later all placed on top of each other and you have a pot, or that's the theory. An hour later I have a base and five long worms. The blessed release bell clangs.

11.30 am

I phone Alison to discover that the gold necklace, the book on Botero, the photographs of Botero oils and a sculpture have all arrived in Cheshire via Bogotá.

3.00 pm

Gym. Once again I manage 2,200 metres on the rower.

5.15 pm

Board meeting. Sergio has been on the phone to Bogotá for the past forty minutes. Armed with a dozen cards (£24) and the judicious use of an illegal pin number, he can now afford to spend an hour phoning Colombia. His brother is waiting to find out if I have any interest in the Boteros. I assure him that as soon as I've seen the photographs I will make a decision.

6.00 pm

I'm writing at my desk when I hear shouting and screaming in the corridor. I leave my cell to investigate, and see half a dozen prisoners standing outside a cell door at the far end of the corridor. I'm told by Darren that the occupant, Danny (burglar) will be released in the morning, and some of his friends wished to give him a farewell present. Half a dozen inmates have filled a black bin liner with water, and added tea bags, sugar, stale bread, butter and beans. They are now all peeing into it. They then empty the contents onto the hapless prisoner's bed just before we are due to be banged up. This ensures that he will have to spend his final night cleaning up the cell if he hopes to be released in the morning.

9.00 pm

Dr Starkey continues his excellent series on the six wives of Henry VIII. Tonight it's Anne Boleyn. Although Starkey spends the whole hour being fairly critical of the queen, one cannot but admire the lady's last sentiment before being beheaded. Her short speech was full of grace, with no fault placed at the door of Henry VIII. She can't have been all bad.

DAY 62   TUESDAY 18 SEPTEMBER 2001

6.00 am

It's been a week since the terrorists struck New York and Washington. It now seems unlikely that any more bodies will be rescued from beneath the rubble, although Mayor Giuliani is a long way off giving orders to stop the search while there's the slimmest hope that anyone might still be alive. He's lost so many firemen, policemen and city workers and was nearly killed himself that I can't see him calling off the search for at least another week; this despite the fact that nobody other than the closest of relatives believes that anyone else can have survived.

8.30 am

Danny, the prisoner who had his cell sacked last night, is now bidding farewell to everyone on the spur as he's due to be released within the hour. He seems to bear no grudges and I watch him shaking hands with Jimmy who tells me later that Danny was probably thankful that his departing gift wasn't physical, as it was on Mel's last night. Jimmy doesn't go into any detail but does admit that Mel had to spend his last few hours on the hospital wing.

9.00 am

Pottery. Carry on producing long worms for my pot, much to the amusement of the other prisoners, all of whom show far more promise than I do. Craig (GBH) is making a horse for his mother, Lloyd (drugs), a heart-shaped jewellery box for his girlfriend, Peter (burglary), another bowl for his aunt and Paul (murder), yet another Christ on the cross.

11.45 am

Call Alison. David's picked up the package from Sale and she has sent the Botero details plus photos to Sotheby's for a realistic valuation, with copies to me. She has also dispatched the Botero catalogue *raisonné* as a gift to the library. At least that way I will get to see the great artist's works rather than have the book confiscated and not returned until I am finally released. Alison has handed the necklace over to James, who awaits my instructions. Still no valuation on the emerald.

6.00 pm

Nothing else worth reporting today, except Jimmy (captain of everything) has just returned from town leave, and looks as if he's had sex. Sex is allowed when you're on town leave. How could they stop it? Jimmy has been out so much recently that he almost treats Wayland like a bed and breakfast motel. Still, to be fair, he'll only be with us for another three weeks. Will he leave Wayland before I do?

DAY 63   WEDNESDAY 19 SEPTEMBER 2001

6.04 am

Things American still dominate the news, as I feel sure they will for some time to come. Tony Blair has seized the initiative and flown to Berlin and Paris for talks with the chancellor and the president. In *The Times* this morning Peter Riddell describes him as having 'a good war', but the truth is that everyone is waiting to find out what George W. Bush's response will be to the Taliban's stonewalling.

9.00 am

Pottery. I finish my masterpiece. My tutor Anne asks the rest of the class to gather round and help her decide what it is. Four opt for a flowerpot, three an upside-down hat, and one inmate feels I should have pressed on and produced an umbrella stand.

11.00 am

Another welcome flood of letters today, including one from John Major and another from George Carey (see opposite). Both are handwritten and full of understanding and kindness.

Lambeth Palace London SE1 7JU

Private   Sept 5ᵗʰ 2001

Dear Jeffrey

Just a personal line, via Mary, to
say that Eileen and I are holding you and the
family up in our thoughts and prayers. What a time
you have been through — and what pain you and
the family here has to endure! All credit to you
all for the quiet dignity you have expressed!

Jeffrey, you are surely proud of
Mary. She gave a brilliant interview on the Today
programme that was shown in the 10.00pm BBC
TV slot. Her attractive composure and articulate

defence was magnificent.

Knowing you, you are putting the time
to very good use. 'Being in prison' is a relative
description. Freedom is primarily a personal
reality — and a person who is free in mind and
heart can transcend the limitations of time and
space and find God's grace where he/she is.

Yours warmly,

George

WEEK COMMENCING

DAY	NO.	MENU CHOICE DINNER		QTY	NO.	MENU CHOICE TEA		QTY
MON	1	BEEF & ONION PIE	H	0	1	CHICKEN & MUSHROOM PIE		0
	2	CHICKEN SPRING ROLL		0	2	PASTA BOLOGNAISE	H	0
	3	MINESTRONE SOUP & BROWN BREAD	VG/LF	0	3	JAMAICAN RICE & PEAS	VG	0
	4	VEGETABLE SAUSAGE ROLL	V	0	4	VEGETABLE CHEESE GRILL	V	0
	5	CHICKEN ROLL SANDWICHES		0	5	HAM BAP - CRISPS - CHOCOLATE BAR		0
	6	CORNED BEEF SANDWICHES		0	6	CHEESE BAP - CRISPS - CHOCOLATE BAR	V	0
TUE	1	HAM & PINEAPPLE PIZZA		0	1	POACHED FISH - TOMATO & GARLIC SCE	LF	0
	2	BEEF & TOMATO SOUP - BREAD ROLL	H	0	2	STEAK & KIDNEY PIE	H	0
	3	VEGETABLE STEW & DUMPLING	VG/LF	0	3	VEGETABLE PASTA & SAUCE	VG/LF	0
	4	CHEESE & ONION FRITTER & BAP	V	0	4	CHEESE & ONION PIE	V	0
	5	CHEESE & PICKLE SANDWICHES	V	0	5	EGG MAYONNAISE SANDWICHES	V	0
	6	HAM SANDWICHES (BROWN BREAD)		0	6	CORNED BEEF SANDWICHES		0
WED	1	CORNISH PASTY		0	1	ROAST CHICKEN	H/LF	0
	2	BEEF BURGER & BAP	H	0	2	ROAST CHICKEN (non halal)	LF	0
	3	VEGETABLE SAMOSA & CURRY SAUCE	V	0	3	VEGETABLE HOT POT	VG/LF	0
	4	TVP PASTA BOLAGNAISE	VG	0	4	VEGETABLE BURGER & BAP	V	0
	5	EGG MAYONNAISE SANDWICHES	V	0	5	TUNA SANDWICHES		0
	6	PORK LUNCHEON MEAT SANDWICHES		0	6	CHEESE SANDWICHES	V	0
		TVP - TEXTURED VEGETABLE PROTEIN				NO. 6 BROWN BREAD		
THU	1	CHICKEN TIKKA PIE		0	1	SAVOURY MINCE BEEF & DUMPLING		0
	2	CHEESE & TOMATO PIZZA	V	0	2	RED PEA SOUP WITH SPINNERS (M/BEEF)	H	0
	3	VEGTABLE AND PASTA IN SAUCE	VG/LF	0	3	VEGETABLE CHILLI	VG/LF	0
	4	LENTIL SOUP & BREAD ROLL	V	0	4	VEGETARIAN SAUSAGE X2	VG	0
	5	CORNED BEEF & PICKLE SANDWICHES		0	5	CHICKEN ROLL SANDWICHES		0
	6	EGG MAYONNAISE SANDWICHES	V	0	6	CHEESE SANDWICHES	V	0
FRI	1	CHEESE BAP		0	1	FISH PORTION		0
	2	HAM BAP		0	2	JUMBO PORK SAUSAGE		0
	3	TURKEY BAP	LF	0	3	CHEESE & ONION SOUFFLE	V	0
	4	VEGAN FILLING BAP	VG	0	4	SAVOURY VEGETABLES	VG/LF	0
	5	VEGETABLE BAP & BREAD ROLL L/F	V/VG	0	5	CHEESE & PICKLE SANDWICHES	V	0
		SERVED WITH CRISPS, YOGHURT,			6	EGG MAYONNAISE SANDWICHES	V	0
		FRUIT & CHOCOLATE BAR				NO. 6 BROWN BREAD		
SAT	1	CHILLI CON CARNE	H	0	1	SOUTHERN FRIED CHICKEN BURGER & BAP		0
	2	LIVER CASSEROLE		0	2	FISH FINGERS X4		0
	3	VEGETABLE PASTY		0	3	BBQ RICE & PEAS	VG/LF	0
	4	VEGETABLE CURRY	VG/LF	0	4	PORK LUNCHEON MEAT SANDWICHES		0
	5	CHEESE & TOMATO SANDWICHES	V	0	5	EGG MAYONNAISE SANDWICHES	V	0
SUN	1	ROAST BEEF &Y/SHIRE PUDD	LF	0	1	CHEESE X2 - BOILED EGG		0
	2	STEAK & KIDNEY PUDDING		0	2	CORNED BEEF X 2		0
	3	PORK CHOP		0	3	MEAT & POTATO PIE		0
	4	VEGETABLE STEW	VG/LF	0	4	CHEESE & ONION PASTY	V	0
	5	CREAMY VEGETABLE PIE	V	0	5	CHINESE VEGETABLES & SAUCE	VG	0

H	HALAL MEAT CHOICE			V	VEGETARIAN CHOICE	
LF	LOW FAT / HEALTHY CHOICE			VG	VEGAN CHOICE	

MON TEA CHOICE 3 AND THUR TEA CHOICE 2 WILL ALL BE HOT OR VERY HOT DISHES

SATURDAY, SUNDAY & MONDAY SWEET NOW CLASSED AS A SUPPER ISSUE, ALTHOUGH 2 SWEETS MAY BE ISSUE

ITEMS ON THIS MENU MARKED WITH AN ^ MAY CONTAIN
INGREDIENTS PRODUCED FROM GENETICALLY MODIFIED MAIZE OR SOYA

THE KITCHEN WILL TRY TO KEEP ALL MEALS AS THEY ARE ON THE MENU.
BUT IF FOR ANY REASON THE MEAL INDICATED CANNOT BE ISSUED A REPLACEMENT MEAL WILL BE ISSUED.

IF YOU DO NOT FILL IN YOUR SHEET YOU WILL BE GIVEN CHOICE NO 1

Mary tells me in her letter that she's been in touch with KPMG who are doing a very thorough job and refusing to be hurried. David Smith, one of their senior partners, plans to come and see me next Monday together with my solicitor. She feels, as I have nothing to hide, that I should agree to the meeting. I had never planned to do otherwise.

12 noon

Lunch. Every day you select a number from the lunch list (see opposite). I always choose the vegetarian option for reasons I have already explained. As I pass Mr Shepperson, he calls out two which turns out to be a beef burger. I point out politely that there must be some mistake. He immediately checks the master list to discover that the mistake is mine. I've circled two, not five. Result? No lunch today. He makes no attempt to offer me an alternative because all the dishes are pre-selected, he explains. In any case, that would set a precedent.

Carl (GBH, goal scorer) who serves the puddings on the end of the line, offers me a second orange and turning to Shepperson says, 'His lordship has never been the same since I introduced him to cannabis.' This is greeted by cheers from the waiting queue. Even Shepperson manages a smile.

6.00 pm

Supper. This time I circled the right number, vegetable hotpot, and, because Mr Chapman is on duty, I end up with two portions.

DAY 64   THURSDAY 20 SEPTEMBER 2001

5.59 am

During the past week George Bush has been criticized – mainly by journalists – for not being able to string a sentence together. But today he confounded his critics (me included) by delivering an elegant and moving speech to Congress. This was not only well written (I read the full text as reproduced in *The Times*), but the speech writer had caught his voice because he delivered the text with such assurance.

Meanwhile the prime minister's timing continues to be fault-less. He flew into New York following talks with Chirac in Paris and then was driven straight to Ground Zero. He was shown round the smouldering site by Mayor Guiliani, before attending a memorial service at St Patrick's.

I tune in four hours later to hear the president's speech to Congress only to find Mr Blair now sitting in the president's box – Mrs Bush on one side of him and Mayor Giuliani on the other. He's done more to strengthen the special relationship in one week than anyone since the days of Roosevelt and Churchill.

8.00 am

Mr Clegg arrives outside my door and stares into my cell. He informs me that the decor, as designed by Shaun, has not met with the governor's approval. The walls must be returned to their original colour by the end of the week. But as the governor hasn't been seen on A block, let alone my spur, in anyone's memory, this seems a little unlikely. However, I go in search of Locke . . .

11.30 am

In my post, among other things, is a catalogue from Sotheby's New York, for their Latin American sale last May. I walk across to Sergio's cell and it's my turn to give him a tutorial. I explain how an auction works, and what is meant by high and low estimates. On the right-hand side of each page is a reproduction of a painting or sculpture. On the left, the artist's name and any known provenance of the work.

We immediately check out the two oils, two sculptures and five drawings by Botero. A sculpture of a reclining woman had a low estimate of $175,000 and sold for $190,000. A vast sculpture of a nude woman had a low estimate of $400,000 but only managed $325,000, whereas an oil painting of a bowl of flowers which had a low estimate of $225,000, sold for $425,000. The five drawings, ranging in price from $15,000 to $25,000 failed to reach the hammer price and were BI (bought in) perhaps because the subject (bull fighting) would not have appealed to many Americans.

We then carefully check the photos of Boteros that arrived in the morning post and try to work out what their low estimate might be, and see if we can spot a bargain. There is a maquette of a nude woman for which I'm willing to offer $10,000, two small oils, $25,000 and $35,000, a large smiling cat, $200,000, and a magnificent portrait entitled *The Card Players* (see plate section) which we settle on at $400,000, although the seller wants a million. My bids are all low, and although Sergio will offer the sellers cash, I doubt if we'll manage to pick up any of them as Botero is, after all, an established international name. However, as Sergio points out, although Christie's and Sotheby's have offices in Brazil, Mexico and Argentina, they have no presence in Colombia, which may provide us with a small edge in an overcrowded market. He also adds that September 11th may have caused prices to fall suddenly. We'll just have to wait and see if he's right.

When 'Lock up,' is bellowed out, I return to my cell.

10.30 pm

I fall asleep dreaming of *The Card Players*. I even know which wall I would hang it on in London.

DAY 65 FRIDAY 21 SEPTEMBER 2001

6.11 am

George W. Bush and Tony Blair officially name Osama bin Laden as the man behind the terrorist attack on the twin towers in New York. Although ships and planes are spotted heading for the Gulf, no one seems to know when any retaliation is likely to take place.

Bush has warned the Taliban, give up bin Laden or we strike. The Taliban's response is that it would be an insult to Allah, but don't mention the fact that the leader of the Taliban is bin Laden's father-in-law. When Bush was told their response he appeared on TV offering $30 million for bin Laden, dead or alive. The moment I heard that I feared for the president's life.

9.00 am

Gym. Alex (special needs group) does three sets of ten sit-ups for the first time and, because he can't speak, gives me a thumbs-up sign, while Robbie and Les applaud him. They are as yet unaware that I will also expect them to begin sit-ups next week. One of the few experiences I shall miss when I leave Wayland (if I ever escape) will be these weekly sessions.

DAY 65

10.45 am

When I return from the gym the newspapers are on my bed. They are so full of news from both sides of the Atlantic that I don't discover until page eleven of *The Times* that the CPS are not going ahead with any assault charges against John Prescott. One or two of the inmates mutter about one rule for New Labour and another for the rest of us. A senior officer is even more appalled by the PM's flippant remark, 'Well, that's John, isn't it?' So much for, 'We'll deal with crime and the causes of crime.'

3.00 pm

Phone Mary, who tells me that the governor has sent all the Prison Service papers showing the stated reasons for my recategorization from D-cat to C-cat.* He wishes it to be known that it is not the Prison Service that is holding up my reinstatement.

She has other news, but not on the phone.

---

* Form RC1 (Adult Male Recategorization Form), dated 31 July 2001, states the reason as: 'Police investigation for allegation of misappropriation of money from the Kurdish Refugee Fund, as advised by the DCI (Detective Chief Inspector) of Police Advisers at HQ.'

DAY 66   SATURDAY 22 SEPTEMBER 2001

11.00 am

Gym. 2,116 metres on the rower in ten minutes; three miles on the running machine in twenty-five minutes fifty-two seconds; and six miles on the bike in ten minutes, making me feel about forty-five, until I see a West Indian replace me on the running machine and do twelve mph for twenty minutes. Still, he is a mere twenty-three.

1.15 pm

I call Chris at the gallery. He's unhappy about the Boteros because he has only black and white reproductions. I agree to do nothing until Sotheby's have authenticated them and come back with a low estimate.

7.00 pm

I call James. He's back in London and tells me that our expert has confirmed that the emerald was a good purchase for $10,000, although he isn't willing to place a value on it. I am relieved to discover that Sergio isn't a crook, and what's more, Mary will end up with a special Christmas present. I wonder where I'll be this Christmas?

DAY 67   SUNDAY 23 SEPTEMBER 2001

12.07 pm

Today is dominated by one incident worth recording in detail, and it all began while I was in my cell reading *The Times*.

I have already explained that during Association a group of West Indians play dominoes in the main room. The amount of noise that emanates from each move would lead one to believe that a heavyweight boxing contest was taking place, which is why a problem arises when a real incident occurs, because the uproar can hardly reach a higher pitch. However, this time the noise was accompanied by the ringing of bells and officers running from every direction towards the Association room. It was like being back in Belmarsh. By the time I made an entrance, the incident was well under control. However, several of the brothers still wished to give me their version of events.

It seems that one of the brothers had been moved from D to A block recently, ostensibly because he had been bullied. It seems that when he was out on a town visit to Norwich a couple of weeks ago, his mates gathered together a large sum of money so that he could pick up an order of drugs. A problem arose when he returned that night and didn't have any of the gear with him. His excuse was he didn't think he'd get the skag past the guards. However, he couldn't come up with a convincing explanation for not being able to return their cash. When he was found cowering in his cell with a cut below his eye and a broken nose, the unit officer quickly moved him across to our block and, they hoped, out of harm's way. However, during exercise yesterday the brothers on D block informed the brothers on A block how he'd stitched them up, and passed the responsibility of exacting revenge on to them.

Back to the Sunday afternoon game of dominoes, where a row broke out with the culprit. One of the players left the group, walked across to the snooker table, picked up a ball, turned round and hurled it at him. Amazingly, he hit the right man in the back of the head at thirty paces (there were eleven prisoners seated around the table at the time). The ball must have been propelled at about seventy-miles an hour, because it split the man's head open. The pitcher ended up in segregation, while the victim is on his way to the local hospital. Both will appear in front of the governor later this week.

The usual punishment would be twenty-eight days added to both men's sentences, which the governor can mete out without recourse to the courts and, in a case like this, an immediate transfer to different A- or B-cat establishments.

I go into great detail to describe this incident simply because those casually reading this diary might be left with an impression that life at Wayland is almost bearable. It isn't. You can never be sure from one moment to the next if your life is in danger. On this block alone there are a dozen murderers, countless thugs and drug addicts with whom I have to co-exist every day.

I'm not unhappy to see my door slammed shut tonight.

DAY 68   MONDAY 24 SEPTEMBER 2001

9.00 am

Legal visit. The governor of Wayland has generously waived the strict rule and allowed two partners of KPMG, David Smith and Alex Plavsic, to join my lawyers so that I can answer questions about the Simple Truth campaign and the accusations made against me by Baroness Nicholson. The five of us sit around a table in the visitors' room and, as the other four are dressed in suits, I feel a little out of place in my jeans and red and blue striped T-shirt.

David Smith is very formal and courteous, addressing me as Lord Archer – something I haven't experienced for the past seven weeks. When the junior partner starts to question me, it quickly becomes clear that they have been very diligent and thorough in their research. They admit they have found no evidence to suggest that I had anything to do with receiving any donations from the public or the distribution of any monies to the Kurds. However, they question me for some time about the make-up of the £57 million.

The Foreign Office has confirmed that it gave £10 million to the campaign, five of which went directly to the Red Cross, the other five to the United Nations. The ODA (Overseas

Development Administration) has also produced documents to show that it can account for a further £38,100,000.

Throughout the world, the Red Cross raised a sum in excess of £10 million at the time of the Simple Truth campaign. Several overseas societies were directly, or indirectly, involved with the concert held at Wembley, organized by Sir Paul Fox, Alan Yentob, Harvey Goldsmith and myself. This event was attended by Princess Diana and John Major, who was prime minister at the time. Mike Whitlam, the then director general, and John Gray, events director, were in charge of fundraising on behalf of the Red Cross. During that period we all seemed to work sixteen hours a day on the five-week campaign, and despite her claims about caring about the Kurds, I don't recall Baroness Nicholson's presence at any function during that time.

By the time you read this, KPMG's full report will have been published. The report will also cover the accusations Ms Nicholson made against that excellent organization – the Red Cross – whose people I watched this morning on TV, working at Ground Zero in New York, searching for bodies, and counselling those in distress. While on the other side of the world, they are on the borders of Afghanistan assisting a million refugees fleeing into Pakistan.

Before Mr Smith and Mr Plavsic leave, they assure me that they will be in touch with DCS Perry at Scotland Yard this afternoon to brief him on their findings. They still have more delving to do concerning Ms Nicholson's other accusations against the Red Cross, but as far as my involvement is concerned, their enquiries are complete.

Once the two accountants have left, Tony Morton-Hooper says he will call DCS Perry and request that my D-cat be reinstated immediately.

I brief Mr Tinkler (the principal officer) on the outcome of my meeting with KPMG and that an announcement is likely to be made in the next couple of days. He confirms that they have been ready to move me for some time, and they are only waiting for a call from the police.

I return to my cell aware that when KPMG finally announce their findings, and the police confirm that they have dropped their enquiries, that the press coverage will be about a hundredth of that created by Ms Nicholson the day after she had appeared on *Newsnight*.

DAY 69   TUESDAY 25 SEPTEMBER 2001

9.00 am

'Burglars.' This is the cry that goes up from fellow inmates when officers appear on the spur to begin a 'spin' – cell search.

I didn't get to pottery yesterday because of my legal visit, and it looks as if I'm going to miss it again today. We've just been told to stay in our cells, as a search is about to be conducted following the snooker hall incident on Sunday. I fail to see how a prisoner throwing a snooker ball at another inmate should result in the whole of A block being searched two days later. However, it's Shane (GBH, gym orderly) who tells me that when they 'spun' the assailant's cell, they found a nine-inch blade hidden under his mattress, and the governor has ordered a comprehensive search of the whole block.

Searching 112 cells takes the duty officers a little over two hours. Mr Shepperson and a colleague spend ten minutes in my cell only to discover that I have two more towels than I'm entitled to and a T-shirt that Sergio has given me because he's leaving on Thursday. They don't comment on these indiscretions as they are obviously looking for more important items.

As I hang around in my cell, I am amused to see the grass outside is littered with different objects that have been thrown out of the windows since the shout of 'Burglars' went up. Apparently it's mainly drugs and other banned substances, but despite a further search amongst the rubbish, no other knives or blades are discovered.

When the 'spin' is over, I'm told that Nigel, (GBH, race relations rep, known as the Preacher – see plate section), has had a carpet removed from his cell, and Darren, two pots of sea-green paint. An officer confirms that no other knives were found on our spur which surprises Darren, although he won't tell me why.

The most common object removed from the cells turns out to be TV remote controls. For some inexplicable reason, remote controls are allowed only on D block (the drug-free block). Result? D blockers trade their remotes for drugs. Prison logic.

12 noon

Exercise. After half an hour of power walking in the fresh air, Darren and I return to the block. As he strolls back through the gate, his eyes light on his two pots of sea-green paint standing in the hallway. I'm afraid I can't resist it. I pick them both up and deposit them back in his cell. He immediately hides them in the dustbin room at the end of the corridor, explaining that should any officer discover they're missing, the first cell they would search would be his, and he could end up on report. If he hears nothing for twenty-four hours he'll feel it's safe to retrieve them. So much happens in prison every day, that it's not unlike a national newspaper. Yesterday's big story is quickly replaced by some new incident demanding the staff's immediate atten- tion. Darren agrees it's the first time I've been able to do something for him.

6.00 pm

I call Will to confirm that he's still planning to visit me on Friday.

He tells me that DCS Perry is off sick and his deputy is unwilling to make a decision while he's away. So much for justice. I begin to think that I'll be in Wayland for the rest of my life.

DAY 70   WEDNESDAY 26 SEPTEMBER 2001

9.00 am

Pottery. It's Anne's birthday. She's amused by my flowerpot (we've all agreed now that it is to be thought of as a flowerpot) and says that it must be left to dry for two weeks before it can be placed in the kiln.

Another of the tutors has brought in a box of crayons for Shaun. When I leave the art room an hour later, I place the crayons in a plastic bag which, to my surprise, the officers don't bother to look inside. I then walk out onto the exercise yard and, in front of several other officers, stroll across to the window of Shaun's cell on C block and pass the crayons through the bars, dropping them on his bed. Only yesterday we were all searched for a knife. Today ... prison logic. I admit I'm only smuggling crayons, but you would have thought someone might have just checked.

2.00 pm

No gym because it's rugby practice. Mr Harley has selected a team of possibles v probables for the first match next week, which he asks me to referee.

The standard turns out to be far higher than I had expected. An Afro-Caribbean inmate picks up a ball that is passed to his toes at full speed and carves his way through a bunch of thugs and murderers to score a brilliant try under the posts. It augers well for next week.

When we return to the changing room the young man tells me that he's never played the game before. How much talent is there in this country that we just don't find out about, let alone nurture?

Another prisoner standing next to me in the shower is six foot nine, and was one of the second row forwards (surprise, surprise). He's more interested in talking about my trial, which he describes as a diabolical liberty. As I never discuss my case with other inmates, I only listen.

'I also got four years,' he said, 'for burglary – with five hundred and two, yeah, five hundred and two,' he repeats, 'other offences to be taken into consideration.'

DAY 71   THURSDAY 27 SEPTEMBER 2001

8.00 am

Sergio will be leaving for Heathrow within the hour. We agree
that I will call him next Tuesday at 7 pm GMT, two o'clock in
Bogotá. He tells me that there is at least £7 left on his BT
phonecard, which ought to be enough for him to let me know
that he has arrived safely and put in my offer for the Boteros.
Could I really get *The Card Players* for $400,000?

9.00 am

Pottery. Shaun spends two hours, with two ten-minute breaks,
drawing Jules's body – in a crouching position, and wearing his
grey prison tracksuit. This is his best effort yet. He'll add the
head next week. He now has only Steve (conspiracy to murder,
library orderly) and Jimmy (Ecstasy and captain of everything)
left to draw. However, as Steve rarely leaves the library, Jimmy is
out all day working on the farm and Shaun is due to be released
in four weeks' time, this may prove a close-run thing. I will not
see the final montage until Shaun has presented his portfolio to
my literary agent, Jonathan Lloyd.

3.30 pm

Exercise. As we circumnavigate the yard, Darren tells me about a prisoner who was transferred to Littlehey early this morning; the governor considered that his life might be in danger if he remained at Wayland. He had already been shipped out of Blunderstone Prison earlier this month when it was discovered that he was being beaten up on a regular basis.

'When he arrived here,' Darren continues, 'he claimed that he was in for punching a taxi driver, which few of us believed. It just didn't add up,' he added without further explanation. By now we've completed two circuits and I'm none the wiser as to what this is all about. But Darren is enjoying keeping me in suspense.

The unnamed prisoner lasted on C block for only a few days before they torched his cell, and set fire to all his belongings, so he was quickly moved to A block. But he lasted only one night before a delegation of prisoners paid a visit to the principal officer (Mr Tinkler), telling him that if the man was still on the block after the weekend, they could not be responsible for his safety.

'What is he in for?' I ask, unable to contain my curiosity.

'Ah, I see I still have your attention,' comments Darren, 'even if I haven't learnt to curtail your impatience.' He pauses dramatically. 'He has committed a crime for which his fellow prisoners would show no mercy.' Darren covers a few more yards before he adds, 'He kidnapped and raped a thirteen-year-old girl. So they've finally moved him to a prison where he will be safe, because he'll only be locked up with other nonces.'*

---

* Nonce – prison slang for not of normal criminal element.

DAY 71

6.00 pm

George W. Bush's first act of war is to sign an order freezing all accounts to which Osama bin Laden has access. It's being reported on the evening news that Clinton attempted to do the same thing when he was president but couldn't get Congress to back him.

Nothing worth watching on television, so I return to the works of Shakespeare. Tonight, *King Lear*. If only the Bard had experienced a few months in prison . . .

DAY 72   FRIDAY 28 SEPTEMBER 2001

9.00 am

Gym. It's my weekly session with the special needs group. I now have my own little class – Alex, Robbie, Les and Paul. We begin on the rower before moving across to the running machine, and this week I ask them all to try sit-ups. A new challenge. Alex and Robbie manage ten, while Les and Paul find it difficult to do more than five. But at least they now have a weekly target.

12 noon

Lunch looks disgusting, so I don't bother. I have a visit today so I can supplement my diet from the canteen.

2.00 pm

Fortnightly visit. This Friday, my three visitors are my son Will and two of my dearest friends, Chris Beetles and Godfrey Barker. I've decided to allocate the first half hour to Will, followed by twenty minutes with Chris, then another twenty with Godfrey and then a final session with all three.

Will starts by telling me about a call he received during the journey to Wayland telling him that the KPMG accountants had just come out of a meeting with the police, and had left them in no doubt that I was never involved with the collecting or distribution of any Simple Truth money donated to the Red Cross. Will goes on to say that he can't believe I'll still be at Wayland this time next week.

Will's next piece of news is that he has a new girlfriend, but as he's returning to America on Thursday, he can't be sure if it's going anywhere. I'm disappointed. I can't wait to be a grandfather. The rest of Will's news is domestic, and after thirty minutes, he makes way for Chris.

Chris appears with a toasted cheese and tomato sandwich – quite the finest delicacy I've eaten for the past seventy days. I'm still not quite sure how he managed it.

I begin by briefing Chris on Shaun (forgery) and the sketches he's working on for this diary. As Shaun will be released in three weeks' time, I've asked him to visit Chris at the gallery and present his portfolio. Chris explains that there's a recognized fee for the reproduction of an artist's work, but if I want to purchase the originals, he will happily negotiate a fair price.

We go on to discuss Botero. Chris feels that as the great man has such an international following the chance of picking up a cheap original, even if Sergio *does* know Botero's mother, seems unlikely. I accept his judgment, but still feel it's possible Sergio might surprise us. Chris shrugs his shoulders. When he changes the subject to Tottenham Hotspur, I quickly replace him with Godfrey.

Godfrey brings me a second cheese and tomato sandwich, not toasted this time.

Godfrey is a distinguished art critic, academic and a friend of twenty years' standing. We discuss an important matter concerning Mr Justice Potts and a dinner Godfrey and his wife Ann attended a couple of years ago, when the judge made remarks about me which, if true, I believe should have disqualifed him from presiding over my case. Godfrey needs to check his diaries before he can confirm the exact evening the supper took place, and the reasons why Sir Humphrey made the remarks he did. Godfrey promises to keep Mary informed. Ann Barker serves on the Parole Board, and another member of the Parole Board was also present at the dinner. Thank God for friends who believe in justice.

The final session spent with all three of them is great fun, not least because Will brings me another cheese and tomato sandwich. I didn't have lunch, and now I needn't bother with supper. Godfrey tells me that he believes IDS can win the next election. Chris pours scorn on the idea, and is happy to stake a Mars bar on Blair, who he believes has hardly put a foot wrong since September 11th.

'Let's see what he looks like in a year's time,' counters Godfrey.

I can only wonder where I'll be in a year's time . . .

The call for visitors to leave comes all too soon, and I am painfully reminded how much I enjoy the company of old friends.

When I leave to return to my cell, I am stopped and made to suffer the humiliation of a strip-search. Two junior officers obviously think it will be fun to tell their friends at the pub tonight that they made Lord Archer take all his clothes off. Good heavens, they discover I have a penis just like other inmates. It spoils what had been a better day. However, their pettiness is not typical of the majority of officers at Wayland.

DAY 72

6.00 pm

Jimmy is back from four days of home leave – this is allowed for non-parole prisoners who have served a third of their sentence. Jimmy's sentence was three and a half years, mine four. Mr Justice Potts understood the difference only too well.* Jimmy says he can't wait to get a good night's sleep. He's had sex with two women in the past forty-eight hours; one stupid but sexy, the other an undergraduate who likes telling her friends she's sleeping with a convict. He can't decide which of them to commit to when he's released in three weeks' time. Darren offers him sage advice: 'If you can't choose between them, neither can be right.'

10.00 pm

For the first time since September 11th the lead story on the *Ten O'Clock News* does not come from the other side of the Atlantic. It still involves terrorists, but this time the report comes from Northern Ireland. I wonder how long the problems of Osama bin Laden will remain paramount, as one can't help remembering that Saddam Hussein is still on the loose . . .

I switch off the news, and continue my Shakespearean marathon by turning to *Richard II*.

---

* If a prisoner is sentenced to less than four years, he is automatically released at the halfway stage, and now can also benefit from four and a half months' tagging. Thus a prisoner with three-and-a-half-year sentence will serve twenty-one months, with four-and-a-half months of that on tag. So he will be discharged from prison after sixteen-and-a-half months. If you are sentenced to four years and above, you have to complete at least half your sentence with no hope of a tag. That is why judges often pass sentences of three years and nine months. If Mr Justice Potts had sentenced me to three years and nine months, I would have been released six months earlier, and not have to endure stiff parole terms when released.

DAY 73   SATURDAY 29 SEPTEMBER 2001

9.00 am

Jimmy now wants to escape. He's due to be released in three weeks' time, but those four days on the outside have given him a taste for freedom. He has no intention of returning to jail. It was Jimmy's first offence, and he swears it will be his last.* I have come to admire the way the Prison Service, the probation officers and the parole board are able to assess which prisoners are likely to reoffend and which are not. They probably make mistakes, which will guarantee them unflattering headlines wishing they had chosen an easier profession. But let's at least be thankful someone's willing to do the job.

11.30 am

During exercise Darren tells me about a prisoner who's been shipped out this morning at short notice. It seems that he was fast becoming the No. 1 drug dealer for the prison, and was happy to exchange his wares – cannabis, cocaine and heroin – for phonecards or tobacco. However, a problem arose because the drug baron on C block was only willing to supply his stock

---

* Currently working on a building site in Ipswich.

for cash, paid into a private bank account on the outside. Let me remind you how this works. Prisoners will instruct a friend or relative during visits (they consider the phone or letters too risky) to place money into an account of an associate of the prison drug dealer, who then supplies the gear.

When the drug baron on C block found his customers were moving their business to the new boy on B block because he didn't require cash, something drastic needed to be done. Yesterday, while his rival was in the gym, he paid two other inmates (cleaners) on B block to torch his cell. Result, the prisoner whose cell was torched was immediately transferred to another gaol. This means that the drug baron on C block is able to continue his evil trade and will be released in a few weeks' time supported by a healthy bank balance.*

8.00 pm

There is rarely anything worth watching on TV on a Saturday night, so I finish off *Richard II* – or to be more accurate, an assassin finishes off the poor fellow. I last saw the play performed at the Barbican with Sam West in the title role. I had been looking forward to his Hamlet at Stratford, but it was not to be.

---

* In fact, he's now back on the outside acting as the supplier for the new drug baron on A block.

DAY 74   SUNDAY 30 SEPTEMBER 2001

8.00 am

I call Mary to be told that the police are dropping their enquiry having not even bothered to interview me.* Mary is thinking of writing to Baroness Nicholson and demanding an apology. I tell her it's a waste of time as Nicholson has neither the grace nor the decency to admit she made a false accusation. Ms Nicholson is a wealthy woman. It would be a noble gesture on her part were she to cover KPMG's costs, rather than leave the Red Cross to foot the bill.

Mary goes on to discuss a conversation she's had with Godfrey. He assured her that he is aware of the importance of any affidavit he might sign, and the effect it would have on my appeal. She also confirms that she is flying to Washington on Thursday, and hopes that by the time she returns the following Tuesday, I will have been moved to an open prison.

---

* Much later, I discover by means of making a 'subject access' request to the Metropolitan Police under the Data Protection Act, that the enquiry was terminated because of 'the lack of evidence from the informant' (i.e. Nicholson). In November, the police and Red Cross issued a joint press release stating that 'no evidence had come to light in relation to these allegations'.

DAY 74

10.30 am

Chapel. The prison has appointed a new chaplain. His name is Nick Tivey and, from his accent, I can only assume he hails from somewhere in the north of these islands. He looks around thirty, and tells me that he's served in two parishes as a priest, before becoming a prison chaplain.

His sermon, or chat, to the inmates is very informal, and more effective for that. His theme is how Jesus despised the Pharaohs (bigwigs) and much preferred to mix with the sinners (us). Applause breaks out among his congregation of seventeen (nine black, eight white), which has doubled since I last attended chapel. He must be doing something right if it's only his second week.

8.00 pm

I begin to read *The Tempest* and am reminded of John Wood's consummate performance as Prospero at Stratford.

> We are such stuff
> As dreams are made on, and our little life
> Is rounded with a sleep

But not tonight, because Shane (GBH, gym orderly) has his TV full on while he watches the Sunday-night boxing. He likes to join in by offering his opinion on each bout, sometimes each punch, at the top of his voice. 'Prick' and 'wanker' are his more repeatable expletives. The boxing ends at 12.35 am, so I must have fallen asleep sometime after that.

DAY 75　　　　　MONDAY 1 OCTOBER 2001

8.15 am

I mention to Shane that he must have kept most of the spur awake until after one o'clock, to which he replies, 'Let's face it, Jeff, I'm a fuckin' yob, and you'll just have to fuckin' well learn to live with it.'

9.00 am

Pottery. One prisoner knocks the trunk off another inmate's elephant and all hell breaks loose. A lot of oaths are uttered as the two of them face up for a fight, while the lifers goad them on. Anne disappears into the next room, and it's some time before peace is restored. I discover later that both inmates involved are due to be released in a few weeks' time, and neither would have wanted their sentence extended. The lifers glower, disappointed by the lack of action.

When the atmosphere returns to near normal, I suggest to the two lads that perhaps they both owe Anne (our teacher) an apology. Two older prisoners, both lifers, look on to see how the youngsters will react. They immediately disappear into the next room and say sorry to Anne. She looks surprised. The lifers nod in my direction. I make no excuses for these two louts' behaviour, but how many of us realize just how lucky we are not to have been subjected to an upbringing where violence, bad language and crime are the norm?

3.00 pm

Three members of the Board of Visitors come to see me. They've heard I'm leaving in the near future, and I wanted a chance to chat to them. The BoV are all unpaid volunteers who give service without a great deal of thanks as both sides of the iron door are sceptical about their usefulness. Almost all the prisoners describe them as a complete waste of space, with the usual adjective attached. This isn't actually fair, because these volunteers have brought about many improvements to prison life over the years, and only last year convinced Jack Straw (Home Secretary at the time) to change his mind on a major decision that affected Wayland.

I suggest to them that perhaps they should appear more often in the exercise yard. Once prisoners get used to seeing them strolling around, they may well come up and have a chat, and that might give inmates more confidence in them. We then discuss several contentious issues, in particular, the daily gripe about being banged up early on a Saturday, Sunday and Monday, when we are incarcerated for fourteen hours at a stretch. They point out the problem of staff shortages. No one likes to admit that there are only four officers on our wing at weekends. Officers at Wayland are currently owed 4,000 hours of overtime between them, and I doubt if it's much different in any other prison.

DAY 76   TUESDAY 2 OCTOBER 2001

9.00 am

The new probation officer asks to see me. Once I've settled in
his office, he explains that he's only going through the motions
because if I move to a D-cat in the near future I won't be seeing
him again. When he learns that I'm appealing against both
conviction and sentence, the meeting comes to an abrupt halt,
and I am sent back to my cell.

12 noon

I phone Alison to discover that Tony Morton-Hooper has faxed
Mr Carlton-Boyce (governor in charge of movement) with my
preferences for a D-cat:*

> Latchmere House, Richmond
> Spring Hill, Buckinghamshire
> Ford, Sussex
> Stamford Hill, Kent

---

* All inmates have the right to name the prison they would like to be transferred
to, usually the one nearest to their family.

DAY 76

They all sound like minor public schools.

I know that they are unlikely to allow me to transfer to Latchmere House as I don't fulfil their criteria,* and Ford has already turned me down on the grounds that they couldn't handle the press interest. The inmates who have been to Stamford Hill tell me it's full of young crackheads who will drive me to an early grave. I expect therefore to end up at Spring Hill, which Mr Meanwell has recommended all along.

3.00 pm

The SO (senior officer) on duty calls me in for a private word. It seems that two prisoners on C block have complained to the governor that I was seen wearing a tracksuit top during exercise, a privilege enjoyed only by enhanced prisoners. He will therefore have to search my cell for the offending article, but he's rather busy at the moment, so he won't be able to do so for another thirty minutes.

The offending article is a cream Adidas top, bequeathed to me by Sergio on the day he was deported. I return to my cell and hand the top to Darren. After I've told him about the interview, he calls in Jimmy, and between them they give my cell a thorough going over. They also remove one bedside lamp, one tin opener and a yellow check blanket, all of which I have acquired during the past month, and am not entitled to unless enhanced.

The SO arrives thirty minutes later, accompanied by another officer and together they search my cell. They reappear fifteen minutes later, declaring my cell to be clean.

---

* Must have completed a quarter of your sentence, and therefore be eligible to work outside the prison.

I later learn that the two prisoners from C block who made the complaint are lifers – both in for murder. Envy in prisons is every bit as prevalent as it is on the outside.

7.00 pm

I call Sergio in Bogotá and take advantage of the £7 left on his phonecard. The news is not good. None of my bids for the Boteros has been accepted. Chris Beetles turned out to be right – knowing the artist's mother is of no significance when dealing with a painter of international reputation. 'Offer $500,000 for *The Card Players*,' is my immediate response. There is a long silence before Sergio admits, 'It's already been sold for $900,000.' Beep ... beep ... beep ... seconds to go. 'I'm sorry, Jeffrey, I'll keep trying to find you a ...'

I've never heard from Sergio since.

DAY 77   WEDNESDAY 3 OCTOBER 2001

8.15 am

As we wait to be called for breakfast, the talk among the prisoners in the corridor is all about Shane (GBH, gym orderly). They're fed up (not their actual words) with the incessant noise he makes late at night and first thing in the morning. I overhear that two or three of them are planning to beat him up in the shower room after he comes back from the rugby match this afternoon. I ask Darren if I ought to report this to Mr Tinkler.

'No,' he says adamantly. 'Mind your own fuckin' business and leave it to us. But when you next see Tinkler or Meanwell, you could mention what a fuckin' nuisance Shane's become. Most of us would like to see him moved back upstairs.' It's the first time Darren has sworn in front of me.

9.00 am

Pottery. Cancelled because I have to attend a meeting with Reg Walton, the sentence management officer. He seems a nice chap, if a little overburdened by it all. He explains that he has to fill in yet another form if I'm to advance to a D-cat.

'Be reinstated,' I explain firmly, giving him a brief run-down of how I ended up at Wayland. He nods, and begins to fill in the little boxes. Here we go again.

Drugs	no history
Violence	no history
Escape (risk)	low
Reoffend (risk)	low
Prison offences	none
Behaviour	stable
Self-inflicted harm (risk)	low
Offences in prison	none

Once he's filled in all the little boxes he stands up, shakes my hand and wishes me luck.

'My wife loves your books.' He pauses. 'Though I confess I've never read one.'

2.00 pm

I referee a rugby match between Wayland and a local RAF camp. It's our first game against a visiting team, and it shows. I play the advantage law as best I can to assist Wayland, but the RAF still end up winning 39–12.

4.10 pm

Mr Tinkler says that he needs to see me following my interview with Mr Walton. Steve tells me that he has never known the two meetings to take place on the same day, which he takes as a sign they will be moving me soon. I've come to learn what 'soon' means in prison, so I don't comment.

DAY 77

6.00 pm

Shane is roaming around the corridor in his dirty rugby kit, avoiding the shower room and being nice to everyone. He even walks across to my cell to congratulate me on how well I refereed the match (frankly, not that well). Darren later tells me that Monster (taxi driver, transporting cannabis) had warned him of his impending doom if he doesn't reform. Far more effective than a ticking-off from an officer.

8.00 pm

I finish *The Tempest* in peace. Shane has got the message, but for how long?

DAY 78   THURSDAY 4 OCTOBER 2001

8.20 am

Meeting with the PO, Mr Tinkler. He tells me that he's signed my D-cat forms, but they still have to be countersigned by my spur officer, Mr Clegg. Mr Tinkler leaves me in no doubt about how he feels the system has treated me. I accept that he and the uniformed staff have done everything in their power to make my incarceration in Wayland bearable, remembering that I was never meant to come here in the first place.

8.50 am

Carl (GBH, servery, goal every match) comes down to our spur to say goodbye. It's always interesting to see how the different prisoners react to someone who's being released. There are those who will be leaving themselves within weeks, even months, who hug him and shake him by the hand, while the long-termers look on sullenly with envy in their eyes.

My abiding memory of Carl will be the day I put on a smart pair of brown loafers when Mary came to visit me, and he said, 'I've got a pair just like those, Jeff. Did you get them in Harrods?'

'Yes,' I replied.

'So did I,' said Carl. 'But I'll bet you paid for yours.'

As Carl leaves, Mr Clarke comes onto the spur and wishes him luck. 'I feel sure we'll be seeing you again,' he adds.

9.00 am

Pottery. My pot, or however we think of it, is drying, so I watch Shaun add Jules's head to last week's shoulders. Jules is pleased with the result and wants the original to give to his mother, always an excellent sign. Normally Shaun would charge £5 or the equivalent in tobacco, but he explains to Jules that my publishers have to see all the sketches first. I promise that, once they have, Jules will be sent the original. (See plate section.)

Jules has already been enhanced, which affords him several privileges, including wearing his own clothes. He's recently come down to our spur to take over Danny's cell. He tells me that they've enrolled him as a Listener which, as I've already explained, is a big responsibility. His educational programme (A level English) is going well, and when he says, 'I won't be coming back once I've been released,' in his case, I believe him.

3.15 pm

Gym. Complete programme in one hour, steady or slight improvement almost every day.

6.30 pm

Mr Clegg takes me through my D-cat form and, as my spur officer, signs me off as a model prisoner. By that he means no drugs, no violence, no other charges since entering prison. The document will now be passed on to Mr King, who in turn will send it up to Mr Carlton-Boyce, who in turn ...

Mr Clegg goes on to tell me that a prisoner has reported him for racism. Now whatever failings Mr Clegg might have, being a racist is not one of them. So when I return to the spur, I brief Nigel (GBH), known as Preacher (see plate section), who is the block's race relations representative. He tells me that he'll speak to Mr King and try to straighten things out.

8.00 pm

Mary has flown to Washington for the fiftieth birthday of a mutual friend, so I can't call her.

I begin *Henry IV, Part I.*

DAY 79   FRIDAY 5 OCTOBER 2001

9.00 am

My little special needs group are now breaking records every week. Alex is even joining in with catchball, which rounds off every session. Darren has promised to take them over once I depart, which is a relief, because he's almost as much of a martinet as I am.

11.00 am

Mr King tells me that my D-cat forms have been handed over to Mr Carlton-Boyce. He also adds that Nigel has been to see him about Mr Clegg, and made it clear that no other prisoner has ever described him as a racist. Mr King thanks me for my intervention, explaining that this sort of slur is hard to remove once it's been written up on an officer's report.

'Tell Ms Nicholson that,' I say in a moment of anger.

12 noon

Lunch. I have a small portion of beans and chips as it's canteen day. How can I hope to lose weight with a diet of beans and chips supplemented by Cadbury's Fruit and Nut plus crisps? I shall have to become the gym orderly at my next prison.

9.00 pm

The prime minister hints that the bombing of Afghanistan is about to begin. He adds that the ground war that will follow could continue beyond next summer. I can only wonder where I'll be next summer.

Manage Act IV of *Henry IV, Part I* before falling asleep.

'If I be not ashamed of my soldiers, I am a soused gurnet,' declares Falstaff. I have to look up gurnet.

DAY 80   SATURDAY 6 OCTOBER 2001

11.00 am

Governor Carlton-Boyce calls for me to confirm that my D-cat is going through the system. He asks if I have any preference as to which prison I would like to be moved to. It becomes clear he hasn't read Tony Morton-Hooper's letter. I explain that as my main residence is in London, any D-cat in that area would be fine, because then my family will find it easier to visit. We discuss Latchmere House, Spring Hill and Stamford Hill. He says he'll check on availability and let me know.

2.30 pm

Amazing Brookes cartoon of Osama bin Laden as a poisonous mushroom in *Nature Notes* on the back of today's *Times* (see plate section). I call Chris Beetles, who represents the cartoonist and ask if we should add it to the collection.

I have been putting together a cartoon collection – with Chris's help – for the past fifteen years, which I had intended to leave to the Palace of Westminster (Parliament). I'm even having second thoughts about that. The collection comprises around three hundred drawings, and includes works by Beerbohm,

Vicky, Gould, Kal, Searle, Furniss, Steadman and Scarfe, amongst many others. The collection also includes sixteen Brookes, but only nine hang in the flat. Chris feels we should remove Hague from the wall (an octopus surrounded by suckers) and replace him with bin Laden. The cartoonist keeps the odd gem for his private collection, so I may not be able to acquire it. Should you be wondering, black and white, £850, colour, £1,450. Chris points out that he hasn't yet seen the quintessential cartoon summing up the full horror of September 11th.

5.00 pm

Steve (conspiracy to murder, librarian) has just returned from the visits hall where he's been in charge of the shop. He tells me that they've had to stop selling Walkers crisps because one of the inmates opened a packet and pulled out a £20 note (the company's latest promotional scheme). The money was immediately impounded by a surveillance officer and credited to the prisoner's canteen account (no inmate is allowed to be in possession of money for obvious reasons). All boxes of Walkers have been replaced with Golden Wonder until this campaign is over.

DAY 81   SUNDAY 7 OCTOBER 2001

8.00 am

After writing for two hours I turn on the news to discover that the bombing of Afghanistan has begun in earnest. Forty strike aircraft and fifty cruise missiles (£750,000 each) have been deployed. David Frost interviews everyone from Kissinger to Clinton, but by 9.30 am we're none the wiser as to how the campaign is going.

11.00 am

Exercise. As Darren, Jimmy and I stroll round the yard we pass an officer I've never seen before because he's attached to another block. His name is Zac Carr, known as 'Z cars'. Jimmy tells me that he was temporarily suspended for allowing a prisoner to tattoo him. It's an offence for one prisoner to tattoo another, let alone an officer. Jimmy then describes how the prisoner (the best tattoo artist at Wayland) goes about his craft. I later ask Mr Nutbourne if the story is true. He nods and says, 'I could tell you many more stories about Z cars,' he pauses, smiles, and adds, 'but I won't.'

11.45 am

Nigel (GBH, race relations rep) walks into my cell to complain that black people aren't represented enough on TV. I sympathize with him and ask what he feels should be done about it.

'They ought to show *Crimewatch* seven nights a week,' he adds with a grin, 'because that would just about even it up.' Having got a rise out of me, he leaves. I continue writing.

8.00 pm

Patricia Routledge gives a moving performance in *Everyone's Nightmare*, the true story of a woman who was wrongly convicted of murdering her mother and spent four years in jail before her sentence was quashed. Once you've been convicted, it can take forever to prove your innocence.

DAY 82   MONDAY 8 OCTOBER 2001

11.00 am

All the papers have stories reporting that I'm about to be transferred to a D-cat. The *Daily Mail* mentions five possible prisons, so that they can eventually tell their readers they got it right. They didn't. None of them bother to say that the police have dropped their enquiries. I suppose that would be asking too much.

12 noon

The allies have bombed Kabul for a second night, but there is still no news as to how effective the onslaught has been.

6.00 pm

Write for two hours, but am unable to concentrate because I know Mary is on a flight back from New York. I won't be able to speak to her until tomorrow morning as I'm already banged up.

8.00 pm

Mr Nutbourne comes to my cell to tell me that he's off on holiday to Cuba. He assumes I'll have been transferred by the time he returns and says that he's sorry to have met me in these circumstances, and wishes me well for the future.

DAY 83   TUESDAY 9 OCTOBER 2001

8.45 am

Mr King tells me as I collect my breakfast that I will not be going to Latchmere House, so they are now trying Spring Hill. As Mr Carlton-Boyce has not briefed me himself but left it to the duty officer, I fear this does not bode well.

11.00 am

Exercise. Darren and I are joined by a prisoner from Singapore, who wishes to remain anonymous. He tells us that he's inside for selling 'duff' heroin to a young girl, who later died in hospital. He was convicted of manslaughter and sentenced to four years. He just thought I ought to know.

5.00 pm

Jimmy has just come back from work and tells me that he saw a lifer being released this morning who had served over twenty years. He was accompanied by nine plastic bags and a double bed that he'd made in the workshop. But he has a problem. No one turned up to collect him, so they had to put him back in his cell overnight. Heaven knows what they did with the double bed.

DAY 84   WEDNESDAY 10 OCTOBER 2001

9.00 am

Pottery. Say farewell to Anne, as I'm fairly sure I won't be at Wayland this time next week. She promises to put my pot in the kiln, and then deliver it to Chris Beetles so that I can give it to Mary for Christmas.*

2.00 pm

Rugby. I referee a match against an army team from Bassingbourne, which turns ugly in the last few minutes of the game. Shane (GBH and gym orderly) runs halfway down the pitch and thumps one of the visiting players. I realize I have no choice but to send him off. I blow my whistle and chase after him, but two officers run onto the field and drag him away before I can reach him. He's immediately banned from participating in any sport for two weeks. The army team beat us by 25–10, which wasn't too bad remembering that we played the second half with only fourteen players on the field. But then I was the referee.

---

* It shattered in the kiln. It's been that sort of year.

DAY 84

6.00 pm

I start reading *Twelfth Night*. I would happily exchange my present abode for a willow cabin.

DAY 85   THURSDAY 11 OCTOBER 2001

8.45 am

Governor Carlton-Boyce tells me that there is no room for me at
Spring Hill, so they are now considering North Sea Camp near
Boston, in Lincolnshire. I point out that it would be a round trip
from London of 240 miles, and I'd never be able to see my
family. Carlton-Boyce doesn't seem that interested and simply
says, 'I'm just doing my job, and that's what I'm paid for.'

9.15 am

Mrs Wendy Sergeant (head of education) has heard that I'll be
leaving imminently and asks to interview me for her PhD thesis
on 'prison reform through education'. As I've only been in
residence nine weeks, and she's served the Prison Service for
eleven years, I'm not sure I have a great deal to offer her, other
than to confirm her worst fears.

I tell her that I believe every prisoner should leave being
able to read and write, and that the weekly pay for education
ought to be at the same level as any job in the prison. In fact,
I would go further and suggest that it would benefit society
more if prisoners received a higher income for agreeing to

participate in education, rather than cleaning their spur, or serving chips.

Wendy tells me that she considers many people are unsuitable for prison and should not be mixing with hardened criminals. She will be suggesting in her thesis the use of halfway houses, especially as the prisons are equipped to handle only 62,500 inmates, with over 67,000 presently convicted.*

2.00 pm

I call Mary to warn her that I'm probably being transferred to a prison over a hundred miles away from London. She tells me that Ramona, my solicitor, has tried to phone Wayland, but the governor is refusing to take her calls, which seems in line with her apparent policy of remaining anonymous.

---

* Home Office statistics for September 2001.

DAY 86   FRIDAY 12 OCTOBER 2001

9.00 am

I turn up at the gym and wait for my little special needs group to arrive. It will be the last time I'll work with them. Without warning, two drug officers appear by the side of the running machine and tell me that my name has come up on the computer for an MDT (Mandatory Drugs Test). Five names come up every day so I can't complain if, after nine weeks, it's my turn. I'm taken to the medical centre to join four other prisoners in a waiting room. Two look distinctly furtive, while the other two appear quite relaxed. When the officer puts his head round the door he asks if anyone is ready. Like a greyhound in the slips, I am through that gap before anyone else can reply.

Mr Kelvin Cross introduces himself and then proceeds to read out my rights before asking me to sign a green form (see overleaf). I ask – for research purposes – what would happen if I refused to give a urine sample or sign the form.

'Twenty-eight days would automatically be added to your sentence.'

I sign the form.

I disappear into the lavatory while one of the officers watches me through a glass pane. After I have handed over my

MANDATORY DRUG TEST AUTHORISATION FORM

Prisoner Name: .... ARCHER ....   **Number:** FF 8282.

┌─────────────────────────────┐
│ Test Reference Number: │
│   │
│ 283 | 01.   │
└─────────────────────────────┘

For allocation when sample is collected

1. The governor has authorised that in accordance with Section 16A of the Prison Act 1952 any prisoner may be required by a prison officer to provide a sample of urine for the purposes of testing for the presence of a controlled drug.

2. You are now required under the terms of Section 16A to provide a fresh and unadulterated sample of urine for testing for the presence of controlled drugs.

3. Authority for this requirement was given by: .... Governor . ...

4. Reason for requirement: (only one box to be ticked)

   [✓] **Random test:** You have been selected for this test on a strictly random basis.

   [ ] **Reasonable suspicion:** You have been selected for this test because staff have reason to believe that you have misused drugs. This test has been approved by a senior manager.

   [ ] **Risk assessment:** You have been selected for this test because you are being considered for a privilege, or a job, where a high degree of trust is to be given to you.

   [ ] **Frequent test programme:** You have been selected for more frequent testing because of your previous history of drug misuse.

   [ ] **On reception:** You have been selected for testing on reception on a random basis.

5. The procedures used during the collection and testing of the sample have been designed to protect you and to ensure that there are no mistakes in the handling of your sample. At the end of the collection procedure you will be asked to sign a statement confirming that the urine sealed in the sample bottles for testing is fresh and your own.

6. Your sample will be split at the point of collection into separate containers which will be sealed in your presence. In the event of you disputing any positive test result, one of these containers will be available, for a period of up to 12 months, for you to arrange, if you so wish, for an independent analysis to be undertaken at your own expense.

7. You will be liable to be placed on report if you:

   (a) provide a positive sample;
   (b) refuse to provide a sample; or,
   (c) fail to provide a sample after 4 hours of the order to do so (or after 5 hours if the officer believes that you are experiencing real difficulty in providing a sample).

Consent to Medical disclosure

* (i) During the past 30 days I have not used any medication issued to me by Health Care.

Signature of Prisoner : .... *Jeff Atcho* ....   **Date:** 12. 10. 01

* (ii) During the past 30 days I have used medication issued to me by Health Care. I understand that some medication issued by Health Care may affect the result of the test. I give my consent to the Medical Officer to provide details of this treatment to the prison authorities.

Signature of Prisoner : ....   **Date:** ....

(*Delete as appropriate)

MDTA/2/97

PRISON SERVICE CHAIN OF CUSTODY PROCEDURE

Prisoner Name: ...Archer...   Number: FF 8282

RANDOM TESTING PROGRAMME

This form is to be used only for tests conducted as part of the MDT random programme
(i.e. where prisoners have been selected by the LIDS computer)

Test Reference Number: 283|01

Checklist for sample collection - tick boxes as you proceed. Refer to guidance notes if in doubt.

1	✓	Only **One** sample collection kit present.
2	✓	Check identity of prisoner. Complete details above and in sample collection register.
3	✓	Carry out search and handwashing procedures. (No soap).
4	✓	Show the prisoner that the collection cup and bottles are empty.
5	✓	Ask prisoner to provide enough urine to be split **equally** between the two sample bottles.
6	✓	*Take temperature using the temperature strip. If temperature is out of range (32-38C) (90-100F), make note in comment section and refer to guidance notes.*
7	✓	Watched by prisoner, transfer urine equally between the two bottles. Fill each above 15ml line and below 30ml line. Press caps on securely.
8	✓	Ask prisoner to initial and date both bottle seals.
9	✓	Watched by prisoner, place a seal over each bottle cap.
10	✓	Dispose of any surplus urine and the cup.
11	✓	Pack two bottles in mailing container and then in chain of custody bag - Do not seal bag.
12	✓	Watched by prisoner, fix barcode labels and enter test reference number on all copies of this form.
13	✓	Ask the prisoner to sign and date the Prisoner's Declaration below.
14	✓	Complete Chain of Custody Report, tear off and place in chain of custody bag facing outwards.
15	✓	Seal bag, ask prisoner to initial bag where indicated.
16	✓	Place sealed bag in secure refrigerator until ready for despatch to laboratory.
17	✓	Allow prisoner to leave.

16528818

Prisoner Declaration

I confirm that
(i) I understand why I was required to provide the sample and what may happen if I fail to comply with this requirement;
(ii) the urine sample I have given was my own and freshly provided;
(iii) the sample was divided into two bottles and sealed in my presence with seals initialled and dated by me;
(iv) the seals used on these bottles carry a barcode identical to the barcode attached to this form.

Signature of prisoner .....Jeffrey Archer.....   Date 12.10.01

sample, I comment that there is no soap in the wash basin. Mr Cross explains that soap added to the urine sample would cloud it, and as a further test is not permitted again for another twenty-eight days, any drugs could have cleared themselves through your system. Can't argue with that either. By the time they've finished with me it's nearly eleven. I return to my cell and make notes on the MDT experience, only disappointed not to have been able to say goodbye to Alex, Robbie, Les and Paul.

1.00 pm

The news is full of riots in Pakistan, anthrax in New York and food parcels being dropped on the wrong villages in Afghanistan. I check my canteen list before spending the afternoon writing.

DAY 87   SATURDAY 13 OCTOBER 2001

2.00 pm

Visit. My son James and our mutual Kurdish friends Broosk and
Nadhim have driven up from London to see me. The talk is
mostly political, and they describe how it feels to live in London
during the present crisis. Nadhim adds that he attended the
Conservative Party conference in Blackpool (he's a councillor for
Wandsworth) and he couldn't help comparing the gathering
with his first conference in Brighton twenty years ago when
Margaret Thatcher was the prime minister.

'Same people,' he tells me, 'they're just twenty years older.'

'You included,' I remind him.

Nadhim's a great fan of IDS, but admits his conference
speech wasn't inspiring.

James is still enjoying his new job in the City and takes me
through a typical day. We then discuss my appeal which doesn't
now look as if it will be scheduled before the new year. The law
grinds slowly . . .

Broosk is full of news, having just landed two big contracts
to decorate large homes in London and Nice. I first met these
two young Kurds twelve years ago – 'Bean Kurd' and 'Lemon
Kurd' – when they helped me organize the Simple Truth campaign, and they have remained friends ever since.

DAY 87

8.00 pm

After a few games of backgammon with Darren and Jimmy I return to my cell to be banged up for another fourteen hours. I've become hooked on *Who Wants to be a Millionaire?*. I would have failed to make more than £2,000 this week because I didn't know the name of the actor who plays the barman in *EastEnders*. However, I was able to answer the £4,000 question, 'Who is the current leader of the Conservative Party? a) Michael Howard, b) David Davis, c) Iain Duncan Smith, d) Kenneth Clarke.' The father and son contestants picked David Davis. Hmm, I wonder if this is an omen or a prophecy?

DAY 88   SUNDAY 14 OCTOBER 2001

11.00 am

I'm called to the hospital wing to fill in some forms to confirm I'm fit to travel. When I return to the spur, Darren tells me it shows that I'm being transferred tomorrow. I find this hard to believe; surely Mr Carlton-Boyce would have warned me. I ask several officers, but as no one has informed them either, I assume Darren must be wrong.

2.30 pm

Exercise. I visit Shaun at his cell window, and talk through what work will be required for this diary just in case I am shipped out tomorrow: one watercolour of the prison, one pastel of a cell, plus drawings of Dale, Jimmy, Darren, Jules, Steve and Nigel. If I suddenly disappear, Shaun promises to deliver them to my agent just as soon as he's released.

DAY 89   MONDAY 15 OCTOBER 2001

8.15 am

Mr Newson arrives outside my cell door to tell me that the
Group 4 van has arrived and is waiting for me in the yard. They
are ready to transfer me to North Sea Camp. He seemed surprised that I haven't been warned. I dash upstairs to see Mr
Tinkler in his office, who confirms the news, and adds that I
must start packing immediately.

'And if I don't?'

'You'll be put on report and may have to stay here indefi-
nitely, and not necessarily on the enhanced wing.'

So much for my so-called 'special treatment', as regularly
reported in the press.

I try to say goodbye to as many inmates as possible – Darren,
Jimmy, Dale, Nigel, Jason, Jules, Monster and Steve. Darren helps
me pack my large plastic bag and then carries it down to the
reception area for me. There are three other plastic bags awaiting
me in reception. They are full of presents from the public –
everything from Bibles to tea towels.

I thank Darren for his kindness and help over the past nine
weeks. He smiles, and offers one last piece of advice.

'Once you've settled in North Sea Camp, contact Doug.* He's the hospital orderly, and can fix anything for you.' I try to thank Darren – inadequately.

The Group 4 guard who will accompany me to Lincolnshire introduces himself as Andrew and kindly carries two of the plastic bags out to the van, so I don't have to make several journeys. To my surprise, I'm to travel to my D-cat in a sweatbox, as if I were a rapist or a murderer. Andrew explains that he has to drop off another prisoner on the way, who is being transferred to a C-cat near Stamford.

'Why are you taking someone from one C-cat to another?' I enquire.

'We're having to move this particular prisoner every few days,' Andrew explains. 'He keeps telling everyone that he's a supporter of Osama bin Laden, and it seems that not every other prisoner is in favour of freedom of speech. However, it still remains our responsibility to keep him alive.'

On the journey to Stamford, the bin Laden supporter demands that the radio be turned up. Andrew tells him that it's quite loud enough already, for which I am grateful, as it's a long, slow trek across Norfolk and on to the plains of Lincolnshire.

I enjoy seeing tall trees and acres of green English country-side, even though it's through a glass darkly. We arrive at the 'bin Laden' prison, where my cohabitant departs. He's hand-cuffed and led away. I can just glimpse him through my little window. A round, colourful hat covers his head, and a black beard obscures most of his face.

We move off again, but it's another hour before I see a signpost: North Sea Camp, one mile. I begin to think about

---

* This also turned out to be good advice, as I took over Doug's job as hospital orderly, while at North Sea Camp.

starting all over again. I'm somewhat fearful. Belmarsh was hell, Wayland purgatory. Have I finally arrived in heaven?

When the van comes to a halt outside the prison, the first thing I notice is that there are no perimeter walls, no razor wire, no barred gates, no arc lights, no dogs, not even any sign of a prison officer. But when I step out of the van, I still feel the terror that gripped me on the first day at Belmarsh, and then again on my arrival at Wayland.

I walk into reception to be greeted by Regimental Sergeant Major Daff, Royal Marines (Rtd).

'We've been waiting for you for fuckin' months, Archer. What fuckin' took you so long?'